Published by Can Scorpions Smoke Change and Creativity
Ltd, London UK via Lulu
ISBN 978-1-291-78683-5

www.stevechapman.org

Steve Chapman is identified as the author of this work.

All artwork in this book was drawn and remains copyright
of Maya Chapman with the exception of a few diagrams and
a shabby cartoon created by her father and some giraffes
drawn by the general public.

Every effort has been made to reference and acknowledge
appropriately those who have had a big influence on this
work.

Permission has been obtained for the inclusion of all
the personal stories included in Chapter 11.

First Edition: April 2014

No scorpions were harmed, persecuted or experimented on
during the production of this book.

Category: Un-Business

Cryptic mystery message: Hi, How are you?

For Maya – who has inspired my creative spirit since the day she arrived.

Contents

The Why? How? and Huh? of this book

Can Scorpions Smoke? An origins story

*Caroline looked like she was pretending to drive a car. She was miming a steering wheel shape and kept moving an imaginary gear stick, so I grabbed two chairs and we sat next to each other. She was the driver and I was the passenger. We sat for a bit and I pulled down the sun visor and looked at myself in the mirror. I fiddled with the glove box and then the electric windows. I realised I was a bored passenger. "How long is space?" I asked. "I mean how long does it go on for and is there an end?" I notice the audience laughing, they seem to like this bizarre question being asked in a rather mundane situation. Caroline responds "What is it with you, you're always asking these questions, can you not just read the map?" Caroline's response suggests that this might not be the first time I have asked an inane question so I accept her offer and ask some more. "How deep is the deepest part of the sea?" There is more laughter from the audience and Caroline responds with more frustration. "Look, I'm not going to go on these long drives with you any more if all you're going to do is ask these stupid questions". I realise that the pattern we have established of my daft and slightly odd questions fuelling frustration, fuelling more daft questions is something special. I fire some more questions. "What is the biggest number?", "How fast is time?", "**Can scorpions smoke?**" The audience laughs, Caroline's frustrations build and I ask myself "Where on earth did that last question come from?"*

My mission is to help turn lives and careers into Creative Adventures. It seems too many people in modern times lament a lack of creativity, excitement and spontaneity in their lives and work and have simply come to accept that this is the way it has to be. I believe that this is a false assumption and anybody, be you a CEO, an airline stewardess or a dustman can find adventure in their lives. The story on the previous page is an extract from my journal written after attending an improvisation workshop in May 2011. I include it in the introduction to this book for a couple of reasons. Firstly, it serves as a sort of origins story as to the genesis of the whole *Can Scorpions Smoke?* thing. You know, like how the first issue of a super hero comic explains how they became radioactive, able to fly or turn people into jelly! After this improvised scene took place, a fellow performer suggested to me that I entitle my MSc dissertation on spontaneity and creativity in business *Can Scorpions Smoke?* which I did. I then chose to also call my blog by the same name and my business is similarly registered at Companies House in London as *Can Scorpions Smoke Change and Creativity Ltd* (which makes letters from the tax man quite amusing!) It now also forms the title of this book.

However, the main reason for including this journal extract is because it tells the story of the moment when I began to see things differently and my own career began to evolve into a Creative Adventure. Those three words came to me in a moment of blankness, a moment when my logical brain had shut down and was no longer present with me on stage. It was a moment when I was in what I could only describe as creative flow. Without conscious thought, the words simply fell out of my mouth and surprised my logical, sensible adult self. OK, it may not be the most profound thing a human being has uttered, but for me it represented a moment where I was able to bypass my internal censor, my rational mind and allow something to arise from a part of me I sensed had been dormant since childhood. It was something that felt like the most obvious thing to say in that moment and, as the words tumbled out of my mouth, I re-connected with possibility and adventure and my own creative spirit was re-awoken!

Ever since that point the question *Can Scorpions Smoke?* has represented my own quest to learn more about this place within me, not by trying harder to be something I am not, but by letting go of some of my adult sensibilities and learned behaviours, discovering what creative wonders lie beneath and exploring how they may serve me well in my life and my work. From that point on I became fascinated about my own creativity and through personal experimentation I managed to liberate myself from many of the ingrained adult patterns and habits I had developed over time, especially during the many years I spent doing a *proper job* in the corporate world. I call this endeavour my Creative Adventure. This book is intended to help others to begin their own.

This book does not aim to answer any questions. In fact, that is an understatement, as it deliberately aims to raise new questions for the reader to  become curious about. My hope is that people will come to this book with questions and leave with at least twice as many - questions about themselves, their lives, their patterns their habits and beliefs and how they might better nurture their creative spirit. Some questions may have intuitive answers, others may take a lifetime of unpacking and experimenting and may never be resolved. This is my aim, as these deeply curious questions are the rocket fuel for Creative Adventures. I encourage you to treat these questions like perpetual Russian Dolls. Inside each question is another question that is slightly deeper and more challenging. The difference between Russian Dolls and the type of inquiry I'm talking about here is it is like a fractal and never ends. Perpetual Russian Fractal Dolls of Creative Inquiry! (Patent pending)

About this book – a serving suggestion

This book is intended as a stimulus and a navigation aid for your own Creative Adventures and is loosely structured in such a way to make that as simple as possible. There are three parts and 11 Chapters that are offered in a particular order as a serving suggestion. However, in the same way that you do not need to arrange your sausages on the plate as illustrated on the packet, it does not need me to say that you can read it however you chose, be that from cover to cover or dipping in and out of parts that pique your curiosity.

To help orientate you to what is on offer, here is a rough guide as to how it is structured.

PART ONE   CREATIVITY LOST AND FOUND
All about the importance of creativity in our lives and our work, how we get in our own way and how we might liberate ourselves from our self-imposed creative shackles.

Chapter 1   Taking Imagination, Creativity and Improvisation Seriously (without making it all too serious)
Explores why imagination, creativity, improvisation and play are growing in importance in our lives and our work and not simply a nice-to-have or something to save for a rainy day.

Chapter 2   Fear, Relationships and Logic
Explores three big individual and cultural factors that seem to inhibit the development of our creative spirit - fear, relationships and logic.

Chapter 3   All You Need is NOW!
Explores the idea that everything we need to become more creative is enfolded in the present moment – we simply need to become more aware of it.

PART TWO   CREATIVE PRACTICES
All about six experimental practices that serve as a stimulus for development and adventure and a lens to make sense of our experiences.

Chapter 4   Mad, Bad and Wrong
Explores our fear of being perceived as mad, bad or wrong by others and how this is probably the single biggest factor in crushing our creative spirit.

Chapter 5   Say "Yes" (to the mess)
Explores what happens if we say "yes" where it would be so much easier to say "no" and how this simple idea can liberate us and kick-start our own Creative Adventure.

Chapter 6   Be Obvious, Be Altered
Explores the idea of being obvious as an alternative to being clever or original, whilst suggesting that if we get better at allowing ourselves to be truly altered by others it can unblock incredible flows of collaborative creativity.

Chapter 7   Fail Happy
Explores how a fear of failure stifles our creative spirit and how getting comfortable with failing happy can open up a whole new world of adventure and learning for us.

Chapter 8   Embody it
Explores what happens if we challenge the dictatorship of our logical brain and let our body and senses take the lead as our spirit guides for Creative Adventure.

Chapter 9   Make Others Look Good

Explores the importance of turning our attention outwards and away from our own needs, placing a greater focus on nurturing the creative spirit of others by giving them permission to shine.

PART THREE   CREATIVE ADVENTURES

All about turning theory into practice, experimentation and adventure.

Chapter 10   Ordinary Stories of Adventure

Explores simple ways in which we can blend these practices into our day to day lives through stories of ordinary adventure told by everyday people.

Chapter 11   Beautiful Imperfection

Explores the perils of striving for perfection when embarking on our own Creative Adventures. A call to embrace our individual flaws as a unique expression of ourselves that we can be proud of, rather than something that we shamefully hide away.

Creative Experiments

A number of experiments are littered throughout the chapters. You can choose to try them out, ignore them, get others to do them or invent your own. The main aim  of these is to encourage us to get into the habit of turning theory into practice through simple, immediate and deeply curious experimentation so we avoid accidentally becoming more theoretical and even less playful. I encourage you to try these experiments in whatever moment you find yourself as you read them. There are only two ground rule to doing them: 1) Be curious and 2) It is impossible to get them wrong! I include some instructions and some questions to provoke your curiosity rather than to lead you to any particular conclusion and remember, you don't need to share your insights with anyone else so just let yourself go. Whatever happens can be your own little creative secret.

A unique synthesis – acknowledgements of my big influences

This book crashes together ideas from the world of Organisation Development & Change (in particular complex social and group dynamics), psychological practices (in particular Gestalt therapy) and the arts, (in particular improvisational theatre). It is a culmination of five years of loosely structured research and experimentation and has many influences that, along-side my own experiences, I have synthesised into this simple and concise offering. I provide some reference notes where relevant and mention all those who have had a hand in its creation in the 'Big Thanks' section at the end, but I wanted to acknowledge the major influences upfront as it is important to me that you appreciate whose voices have influenced my work as you read the book.

Firstly to those in the world of improvisational theatre: Keith Johnstone has been a major influence from the very beginning, through his two books "*Impro*"[1], "*Improvisation for Storytellers*"[2] and through time spent with Keith in London between 2012-2014. Three other improvisers have also been key in helping me experiment with and formulate these ideas: Neil Mullarkey of The Comedy Store (London) and John Cremer of The Maydays (Brighton) both helped me find and then learn from the edge of my comfort zone and Jazz pianist Frank Barrett brought much stimulation through his historic work with Ashridge Business School and his book " *Yes to the Mess - Surprising Leadership Lessons From Jazz.*"[3]

Secondly to those who write about organisations as complex social processes, in particular Patricia Shaw, Ralph Stacey, Bill Critchley and Caryn Vanstone. Each of these has been a big influence in deepening my interest in and understanding of this important body of research either through their excellent written work or through hanging out and working with them in person. Each has helped me make more sense of the organisational and social elements of my research.

I also want to acknowledge my friend and colleague at On Your Feet, Robert Poynton, who straddles both sides of the business/arts equation, provides constant support and challenge to my thinking and whose book "Everything's an Offer"[4] remains a key influence. Finally I want to acknowledge Khurshed Denhugara, co-author of *"The Challenger Spirit"*[5], whose unique blend of intellect, passion, curiosity, challenge, friendship and support has given me the hope and ambition to see this project through to completion.

Finally, before we begin

The on-going, emergent and experimental nature of my approach to research and writing means that my thesis is alive and continually evolving and changing on a day-to-day basis. At times I am excited by it and full of enthusiasm, other times I am deeply frustrated at how difficult it is to write about this subject in a way that models the rather amorphous, messy nature of creativity. However, that's what makes it such an exciting life-long inquiry. This book is intended as a launch pad for your own Creative Adventure, be that in your work, with your family, with friends or even a secret set of experiments that you don't tell others about.

The most important thing is that you take it wherever it takes you.

Steve (London, March 2014)
www.stevechapman.org

Why, How and Huh? References

1 Keith Johnston (1981) *"Impro - Improvisation and the Theatre."* London: Methuen

2 Keith Johnston (1999) *"Impro for Storytellers."* London: Faber & Faber

3 Frank Barrett (2012) *"Yes To The Mess: Surprising Leadership Lessons From Jazz."* Boston: Harvard

4 Robert Poynton (2008) *"Everything's an Offer: How to do More with Less."* Portland: On Your Feet

5 Khurshed Denhugara & Claire Genkai Breeze (2011) *"The Challenger Spirit: Organisations that Disturb the Status Quo."* London:LID Publishing

PART ONE

CREATIVITY LOST AND FOUND

Chapter 1   Taking Imagination, Creativity and Improvisation Seriously (without making it all too serious)

"We don't stop playing because we grow old; we grow old because we stop playing."   George Bernard Shaw (1856-1950)

I remember fondly my boating holiday on the Norfolk Broads with my wife Nancy. The ripple of the water, the sunshine and the grassy banks. It was a welcome break from my incredibly stressful job as the UK's leading neuro-scientist. That was until we reached THAT lock! I  *was very polite to the Lock Keeper but he was very quick to inform me that he was a fully paid up union member, "working to rule" as part of some on-going industrial relations dispute and would only let us pass through when he was ready. Somehow, the Lock Keeper found out what my job was, maybe he overheard my wife making a joke that it didn't take a brain surgeon to operate a lock! Whatever it was, it seemed to enrage him. "So you think you're better than me do you pal? Just because you're a brain surgeon or whatever doesn't mean I'm going to flout union regulations for you!" I remember him saying in a rather aggressive tone. No matter how much I pleaded that I was just a normal guy trying to have a relaxing holiday without any illusions of grandeur or status he became more and more angry. The situation worsened when one of his burly colleagues from the next lock upstream heard the commotion and joined in with his own tirade. Before I knew it our boat was surrounded by more and more angry, unionised Lock Keepers shouting and berating my wife and I. I felt my stress levels building intensely and all I could find the energy to do was to rock back and forth on my knees with my head in my hands, almost sobbing, wondering what had happened to my peaceful holiday.*

Purposeful play

I remember fondly playing the neuro-surgeon in one of my regular improvisation classes. It was a fun scene to play and a wonderful example of how a bunch of people creating stuff together in a supportive environment can transform into a delightful story full of drama, intrigue and laughter. The thing is, whilst the story was a fantasy as a result of our collective improvisation, the emotions, the stress, the anguish and the anxiety I felt as more and more burley Lock Keepers arrived in order to ruin my much needed holiday was very real. I was able to let go of the fact that this was play and immerse myself in the situation as if it were real life, noticing and then using my genuine emotional and somatic responses to help inform me what to do next. I took my own experience seriously, paying attention to the entirety of my here-and-now awareness as a rich source of learning about myself and others. I was able to silence the adult voice in my head telling me that it wasn't real and that I was being stupid, crazy or immature and respond from a much more relaxed and deeply creative place.

This was just one of many developmental experiences I have had through experimenting with creative disciplines such as performance improvisation. It wouldn't be an exaggeration to say that I have learnt more about myself in this way than from many years of formal eductaion at school or in business. For me, the key difference between my formal education and training and these more random, artistic experiences has been that I have learnt not through digesting and regurgitating the words of others, nor by hypothesising and theorising, but through experimentation, play and discovery. Through these experiences I have come to believe that learning is far *stickier* when it is discovered instead of delivered.

In her book *"Workplace to Playspace"*[1] Pamela Meyer describes our early experiences of play as a place *"where we develop a sense of ourselves, experiment with different roles, become socialised, build confidence and explore our creativity. However we get the message [early in life] that play is free and to be set aside when there [is] something important to do."* It seems to me that play is a forgotten art form in the adult world, particularly in modern business. Years of conditioning, from the age of around six or eight starts to force an artificial split between work and play until we forget that the reason we used to play so much was because it was fun and we learnt stuff about ourselves and others. I often wonder how this split became so dominant for me and have worked hard to try and collapse the difference between work and play in order to find a more exciting, energising and life affirming middle ground.

Creative Adventures

The first step in liberating our creative spirit is to experiment with prizing open the fruitful, exciting and sometimes scary overlap in-between work and play, not only recovering play as an essential part of our own work and personal development but  mentally reframing the idea of our life and our work as a Creative Adventure – a state of being in which we feel more alive, more creative, less anxious about the unknown and see possibilities and opportunities everywhere we look. The late Apple boss Steve Jobs once said "*Your work is going to fill a large part of your life and the only way to be truly satisfied is to do what you believe is great work. And the only way to do great work is to love what you do. If you haven't found it yet, keep looking. Don't settle."* It is the quest to discover and perpetually explore this place where work and play overlap as one that I call my Creative Adventure.

Prior to my *Can Scorpions Smoke?* moment I was focused on *career* – something I perceived as a step by step process within which I would follow a pre-determined path to achieve different roles with greater responsibility, impact and reward. Whilst I have always enjoyed my work, I felt that there were boundaries as to what was possible for me, so became rather myopic as to the possibilities that perpetually surrounded me. However, when I came up with the idea of my work becoming an *adventure* I noticed that it had a very different feel to when I considered it a *career*. It felt more alive, more mysterious, more curious, more energising. For me the word *adventure* has given a different meaning, purpose and quality to life itself. I have a real fondness for the children's cartoon *Adventure Time*, a beautifully animated series about a boy called Finn and his dog Jake who have adventures in a wonderful, colourful and often-surreal fantasy world. I enjoy this programme because it is creative, lively, exciting and unpredictable and for me it captures exactly what adventures are about : A deep, child-like *curiosity* that drives one to continually ask the question *"I wonder what would happen if..?"*, perpetual *experimentation* to test out and challenge the boundaries of perceived possibility and using these curious experiments to cause positive *disturbances* to the world around us.

$$\partial = ? + \nu\!\int\!' + \triangle$$

ADVENTURE = CURIOSITY + EXPERIMENTATION + DISTURBANCE

Creative Adventures are about working out ways to bring this formula to life in our own lives and careers in a way that begins to blur the lines between work and play, where we find ourselves experiencing a far more fulfilling and joyful day to day experience. When we begin this journey we start to realise that the artificial separation we make between work and play isn't a real constraint but a social construction – a culmination of dominant personal and cultural patterns as to the nature of work that have emerged over many years and have been introjected to such an extent that we believe them to be actual rules. The fact that they aren't real means they can be perpetually challenged and changed. However, whilst this is true, the social challenges of bringing more creativity, play and personal experimentation into our lives shouldn't be underestimated and it seems to me that the most tricky place to challenge this artificial split is in the corporate world. Those who are able to artfully find a way of turning their careers into Creative Adventures find themselves better able to tap into a long forgotten skillset that not only brings new meaning to their work but also develops some marvellous leadership, change and innovation skills In short, personal and corporate creativity isn't a nice to have – it is a competitive advantage!

Corporate creativity

The economist J.K. Gailbraith once said *"The sole purpose of economic forecasting is to make astrology look credible."* Never before has the uncertainty he was alluding to been so present in our personal and business lives. I'm not really convinced that, as many business leaders assert, the pace of change is increasing (due to my beliefs that change is a natural and perpetual phenomena) but there certainly seems to be a dramatic increase in connectivity as well as a multitude of volatile and lively economic, environmental and societal trends that are making uncertainty more of a norm. The arrival of disruptive technologies, such as social media, are also making the flow of meaning, information and differences of opinion far more rapid and connected and it seems to me that it is no longer leaders who are good at predicting and controlling who are going to thrive in the future but those who are also masterful at adapting.

Despite these trends, I'm yet to come across an organisation that has imagination, creativity or improvisation specified as critical leadership capabilities. The closest I typically find is *flexible thinking*, *entrepreneurship* or *innovation* but without an ability to imagine, be creative and improvise it is virtually impossible to develop these capabilities. I fear that in an attempt to make our language about leadership sound more grown-up and corporate we miss the point that the underpinning capabilities required to think flexibly, entrepreneurially and innovatively are, by their very nature, more artistic, responsive and child-like.

Taking improvisation seriously

Simply put, improvisation is INTENT + ADAPTATION and, in my own opinion, an essential life and leadership skill. Leaders who are able to improvise are able to use their well developed strategic, financial and commercial skills  to form a bold intent, a compelling vision of the future and, at the same time, are able to maintain a deep awareness of the here-and-now that enables them to adapt, change and respond appropriately in the moment. They are able to lead *of* a unique moment in time and not *in spite of* it. Those who lack an ability to adapt continue to adhere to their strategic plan in spite of new information or the emergence of unintended consequences, their original intent rapidly goes past its sell-by date and their people and their organisation suffer. At the same time, those who lack the ability to form a bold intent also lack the ability to form a compelling vision to inspire others and anticipate future possibilities. It is therefore a combination of *intent* and *adaptation* that is required in order to navigate the complex, messy reality of our organisational worlds, however it is the latter of these two qualities that appears atrophied in many leaders.

This is problematic as our organisations are not *things!* They don't have a shape, a density or a boundary and we cannot move them from A to B or change their physical form. Sure, there are *things* within our organisations that we can manipulate and control and simplified maps of what is *supposed* to happen that we can change (e.g. organisation charts, policies, procedures) but not the organisation itself as it is essentially a complex pattern of human beings relating to each other in a way that is as predictable as it is unpredictable. However, the majority of our business education seems to train leaders and managers to engage with their organisations as if they are *things. Things* to be controlled and manipulated as opposed to thinking of them as social patterns that can only be influenced and participated in. Social patterns that are as predictable as they are unpredictable, in which leaders may be in command but are certainly not in control, making an ability to flex, improvise and adapt a critical leadership skill.

Taking imagination and creativity seriously

Being able to respond imaginatively and creatively is key in learning how to improvise, adapt and think flexibly. it is also critical when it comes to an essential component of any modern corporate strategy - innovation. A stand-alone innovation process, department or competency framework starves and becomes stagnant without a truly liberated creative culture to feed it novel concepts to be developed into prototypes or experiments. Similarly, an artificially engineered creative culture lacks spark and energy without permission to imagine and dream at work. In his book *"Out of our Minds"*[2] Ken Robinson describes innovation as *"applied creativity"* and creativity as *"applied imagination"* and emphasises the importance of taking a holistic approach to developing these capabilities in order to unblock frustrated innovation efforts in organisations. Whilst one could argue that trying to label and package these rather more amorphous processes into boxes on a flow chart is also counter-productive, I find the definitions a helpful navigation aid in starting to change conversations about what is really required in order to nurture a more inclusive, creative organisational culture where everyone has the potential to innovate.

Taking play seriously

 My personal campaign is to encourage us to take the development of and investment in these more artistic, amorphous capabilities seriously but, in doing so, to not make it all too serious. I have nightmare visions of swathes of metrics and logic driven dashboards that measure the amount of imagination a company has or a group of very serious, stressed-out looking executives debating the fine detail of how they are going measure a tangible return on investment for their improvisational development! Important does not need to equal serious and simultaneously nurturing an ability to develop these capabilities in a playful way is essential to their development. Pamela Meyer makes a call to shift our perception of our workplace to being a playspace – a place that is still highly productive but far more engaging, relational and developmental for us. *"From workplace to playspace is an invitation to shift from a mind-set that conceives of work as separate from dynamic engagement to one where the workplace is a playspace for new ideas, perspectives and possibilities – to embrace our organisations as living, breathing, ever-changing systems and reclaim play as an essential dynamic of success."*[1] It seems to me that play is a long forgotten developmental art form in the corporate world but one that is key to stimulating imagination and creativity.

A reunion with our creative selves

Discovering or re-activating our imaginative, creative and spontaneous capabilities is not like riding a bike! We can't simply go on a training course that teaches us how to be creative and we're then creative for ever more! We need to develop and commit to an on-going practice or else our newfound abilities begin to rapidly erode as we go about our lives in an overly parental world that is often reluctant to value them. The cultural devaluing and dampening of our creative spirit is most evident as we progress from childhood to adulthood, through education and into work. In his wonderful book *"Orbiting the Giant Hairball"*[3] Gordon MacKenzie tells of his experience of visiting American schools to talk about art and asking the children if there are any artists amongst them.

"The pattern of responses never varied. First grade: En Masse the children leapt from their chairs, arms waving wildly, eager hands trying to reach the ceiling. Every child was an artist. Second grade: About half the kids raised their hands, shoulder high, no higher. The hands were still. Third grade: At best, 10 kids out of 30 would raise a hand. Tentatively. Self-consciously. By the time I reached the sixth grade, no more than one or two did so and then only ever-so-slightly – guardedly – their eyes glancing from side to side uneasily, betraying a fear of being identified by the group as a 'closet artist'."

When I first read this paragraph in the opening chapter of MacKenzie's book I could see my own school life being replayed before my eyes. I remember being highly imaginative, creative and spontaneous at primary school but then less so in the first year of secondary school and by the time I left I had decided, as a result of my own experience and the deliberate or accidental discouragement of others, that these skills were not going to be of use to me anymore. I went into the world of work feeling rather lost and stupid as the things that I had regarded as natural talents and abilities were of no apparent value to potential employers. I decided to begin seeking out more logical, objective and traditional business training and education to fill a perceived gap, hiding my creative abilities away behind a metaphorical wardrobe. It would be easy for me to blame my teachers, parents or employers for colluding over the devaluing of my creativity but, as MacKenzie suggests, *"It is not a plot, [it is] an innocent casualty in society's efforts to train children away from natural born foolishness."*

With this in mind, I believe that we never lose our ability to be wildly imaginative, creative and spontaneous – we simply put these capabilities in a deep freeze. This deep freeze process occurs gradually as a result of a number of factors: we are told that creative subjects are less important than core subjects, we get rewarded and recognised for our logic, deductive reasoning and mechanistic thinking and employers are seemingly willing to pay more for less creative jobs. All of this is reinforced through our own maturing adult beliefs, our peers, parents and other authority figures and then handed down through the generations. I don't believe that this is necessarily as a result of an evil, anti-creative conspiracy but simply an accidental social pattern that is worth paying close attention to.

 I like to imagine every adult going about their day-to-day lives with a little frozen creative genius buried deep inside them that they are largely unaware of. I find this idea incredibly exciting! What if we were able to liberate the little creative genius inside of us? What if we were able to recover only the most useful childlike abilities (leaving behind some of the less positive individual and social attributes of being a child) and combine them with our adult sensibilities and life experiences? How would we go about our lives differently? How would our leaders and our organisations change and evolve? How would society transform? If you are as excited as me about the potential in these ideas the immediate question that comes to mind is how do we start the difficult process of defrosting? The key is to begin to tackle head-on three major human, instinctive traits that seem to inhibit creativity and keep our little geniuses frozen...FEAR.......RELATIONSHIPS.......and LOGIC!

Chapter 1 References

1 Pamela Meyer (2010) *"From Workplace to Playspace: Innovating, Learning and Changing Through Dynamic Engagement."* San Fransisco: Jossey-Bass

2 Ken Robinson (2001) *"Out of Our Minds: Learning To Be Creative."* Chichester: Capstone

3 Gordon MacKenzie (1996) *"Orbiting the Giant Hairball: A Corporate Fool's Guide to Surviving with Grace."* New York: Penguin Group

Chapter 2   Fear, Relationships and Logic

"The only thing we have to fear is fear itself."

Franklin D. Roosevelt (1882-1945)

I was feeling a little weary when I awoke on the Thursday morning. It had been a fantastic week but the lack of sleep, multiple workshops and the moreish festival ale had sapped my energy a little. Today was the last day of the festival[1] and I was scheduled to run a creative workshop. I felt I needed something to get me in the zone, so I had a browse of the early morning outdoor activities on offer. A wild swim? Canoeing on Lake Windermere? Then I noticed something called The Pamper Pole. As we drove to the venue in the minibus I asked the driver about the pole and he explained that the reason it was named "Pamper" was because it was so tall that one might need a nappy when standing at the top! An hour later I was strapped to a harness at the bottom of what was essentially a 30ft telegraph pole with climbing rungs attached to the side. The challenge was three-fold: 1 - climb the pole, 2 - stand on top of the pole and 3 - leap from the pole and hit a ball suspended some seven to eight feet away. I began the climb, which was easy enough, but when I reached the top rung I suddenly realised with horror that, as there was nothing else to hold onto above me, the only way to get myself onto the small disc of wood at the top was to use a combination of my own balance and leg strength. I managed to get my first leg onto the top and realised the second was going to be even more difficult and

require even more strength and balance to stop me from falling. At that moment I remember my whole body vibrating, my heartbeat racing in my chest and my instincts taking over. Just before I made my next move and ever so gradually lifted myself onto this tiny platform in the sky I remember thinking to myself......"NOW I remember what fear feels like!"

Battle of the brains

I must confess, if it wasn't already obvious, I am not a neuro-scientist, I merely played one in an improvised scene once. I also confess that I do like simple pictures and explanations that help me make sense of complex things such as brains! With this in mind, the way I understand the make-up of human beings is that we essentially have three brains that, throughout evolution, have grown on top of each other to make the weirdly shaped, grey jelly-like thing that sits in our skull. Each part of the brain has a proper scientific name but are often nicknamed the lizard brain, the mammalian brain and the human brain and each has a specific role in helping us survive and thrive as a species. Only human beings have developed these brains in such an extensive way and it is the combination of the three that sets us apart as incredibly unique from other species. (That and opposable thumbs I guess. I am also not a mammalian digit evolution expert!)

This over-simplified description of the brain will no doubt have many who know more than me shaking their heads and tutting loudly on the train or in the coffee shop! However, the complex make-up of the brain isn't really something I'm intending to talk about here. What I am interested in is the extent to which the basic, instinctive prime directives of each brain unintentionally stifle our creativity moment by moment. Through getting to know these prime directives better we can begin to understand how our creativity is inhibited by an instinctive need to protect ourselves and to survive in community with other human beings. Through becoming more aware of this we can stop giving ourselves a hard time for not being as creative as we want to be as we are simply programmed this way and acting on instinct. We just need a little re-wiring!

Fear – The Lizard Brain (the reptilian complex)

Our lizard brain plays many essential roles in preserving our basic survival needs. It has three prime directives - eat, reproduce and avoid death and our in built fight-or-flight response associated with these  directives is triggered by what we label as danger or fear. Our extreme response to fear results in our fight-or-flight mechanism kicking in and we shut down all non-essential thought processes and our peripheral awareness in readiness to run away quickly or prepare to attack.

What I felt at the top of the Pamper Pole was the uncontrollable, instinctive, adrenaline driven response to a situation in which my prime survival needs were apparently under threat (even though there was a harness and I was unlikely to die, it didn't seem to make any difference at that precise moment). I included the story of the Pamper Pole at the start of this chapter as I realised that my experience of fear 30ft in the air was very different to other times I have felt a sense of fear when working with a new team, trying out a new workshop experiment, working with somebody very senior or influential, giving a conference talk or speaking up in a group to share my thoughts ideas or questions. In these situations my survival wasn't under threat but I still had an emotional and physical response that I would label as fear. What the Pamper Pole experience helped me realise was that this type of corporate performance fear is very different to survival fear and should probably be more accurately described as social anxiety. Social anxiety is where what is at stake isn't one's survival but one's sense of identity and social standing in relation to others. In other words, it is a relational fear that we often confuse with a life-threatening one. (I've read that our amygdala cannot distinguish between the two, so it seems this is a biological as well as a social challenge!) Getting to know and make friends with this social anxiety lies at the heart of rehabilitating our creativity and is something I continue to experiment with on a daily basis. In my experience, making friends with this fear doesn't mean that it necessarily goes away, it just means one begins to recognise it as being something different to the life threatening fear we often seem to confuse it with. This extra layer of awareness gives us more conscious choice as to how we respond to particularly challenging or unfamiliar situations. We become better able to separate the sensation from the habitual label we assign to it and therefore its meaning subtly changes. Asher Rickayzen, a friend of mine and a partner of Relume Ltd (www.relume.co.uk) describes this process as: "*learning to move from seeing anxiety as a sign that things are going wrong to seeing it as a sign of a breakthrough or possibility.*"

I'm intrigued by the phrase "*leap then look*" – a twist on the sage advice to "*look before you leap*" as a way of encouraging myself and others to become a little braver when it comes to being more creative, experimental and adventurous. For me, leaping before looking has resulted in a number of new adventures and experiences. It has encouraged me to say *"yes"* to stuff before I've had the chance to evaluate it and convince myself it isn't a good idea and has led to some exhilarating, scary and fascinating learning experiences. It has encouraged me to trust my gut instinct and spill out my spontaneous thoughts before running them through my internal self-censor, resulting in some insightful and some nonsensical spontaneous outbursts in groups, some of which have been more helpful than others. Most profoundly, this new mantra has shortened the time between idea and action - coming up with new experiments and trying them out as soon as possible (Most recently, I co-facilitated a creative workshop dressed as a pirate, leading early years school teachers through a series of make-believe high-seas adventures inspired by a children's book - I would have talked myself out of doing this if I'd thought about it too long!)

Leaping before looking is about taking a trustful leap of imagination, curiosity or adventure and only then taking a look at the environment and reactions of others where one has metaphorically landed. I have found it a good mantra to help short circuit the social anxiety that keeps us safe and certain but also keeps us stuck and stale. When I'm running personal development workshops, the experiences I lead people through are designed to help participants feel what it is like to leap and then look, something that is counter-intuitive in most business situations. Often they find the experience terrifying. Then, over time, they make friends with those feelings and start to regard them as valuable resources. Some even find them addictive!

I am, however also aware of the  potential perils of leaping then looking and the reasons why some wise man/woman originally suggested that looking before you leap was a good idea. I am reminded of a story Gordon MacKenzie tells in *"Orbiting the giant Hairball"*[2]. One day Gordon was walking along the cliff tops in San Diego, heading towards the cliff edge in order to find a way down to the beach when he came across some signs saying DANGER! STAY BACK – UNSTABLE CLIFF! NO BEACH ACCESS! Being curious and seeing others on the beach he decided to adventure anyway, dropping down on the ledge below and then onto the ledge below that. It was only when he got half way down that he realised that the next ledge down wasn't visible – he'd have to jump and hope that it was there. He then also realised that he couldn't get back up the way he'd come down! He was stuck and the only way down was a literal leap of faith. He chose not to take a chance and focused on trying to summon help. Eventually he managed to raise the alarm by shouting at the people on the beach and was rescued (and severely reprimanded) by the coastguard. As the helicopter lifted him away from the cliffs he realised that the ledge below was at least 40ft away – had he jumped it would have resulted in serious injury. He also realised that 100 yards further up the beach were some steps! This was a case where looking before leaping was a very good idea.

So, as with most things, it is a balance that needs to be struck here and the way to start to strike a more creative equilibrium is to reflect on where our inaction is really is driven by fear and a chance of death or serious injury versus where it is simply a manifestation of our own unique social anxiety. When it comes to creativity, especially in the workplace, it seems our lizard brain mis-associate the risks of leaping in with a new idea, concept or experiment with the risk of actually leaping from a cliff into the unknown! To learn more about this I decided to conduct a personal experiment. I decided that, whilst I would continue with my *leap first* philosophy, I would also reflect on what my *must look first* list would look like – a list of things where it would be very wise to evaluate a situation before throwing myself into it.

Below is my first ever *must look first* list that I wrote in early 2013.

Must look first...

① ...if there is a real chance of death or physical injury to myself or others (including animals)

② ...if there is a real possibility that my actions may accidentally manipulate, suppress or disempower others

③ ...if there is a real possibility that others may suffer disproportionately to me (exposure to stress, trauma, loss of security/safety (etc)

④ ...when I notice my gut feel is stronger than usual in saying it really isn't a good idea and it feels like I'm doing something to be clever rather than curious.

After I wrote this list I was surprised as to how short it was – four things! Fair enough, if I gave it more precise, logical thought I might talk myself into evolving it further but I trusted my initial gut feel had teased out the major things. I was also struck that most of the things that I tend to hold back from doing on a day-to-day basis because they feel so risky wouldn't qualify for my *must look first* list! (e.g. running a strategy workshop in a highly experimental way using Dr Seuss books as a guiding agenda isn't likely to kill, maim or cause undue suffering – so why on earth am I procrastinating instead of experimenting?)

Of course, even if something *is* caught by my *must look first* list it doesn't mean that I won't ever do it, it simply means I will employ a check step/pause for reflection before leaping to action. Without a huge amount of planning and training and looking first Felix Baumgartner wouldn't have leapt from the edge of space and stretched the boundaries of what human adventure can look like.

Experiment: Must look first lists

- *Take some time to reflect on and write down what is on your own personal Must Look First list – a list of absolutely critical criteria that, if met, mean you must evaluate before taking action.*
- *Think about all of the things that you want to do in life and list them on another piece of paper. These could be short-term activities and actions, long term hopes, dreams and ambitions or simply things you have been procrastinating over for a while.*
- *Look at your list through the filter of your must look first criteria. How many of your activities, actions, hopes, dreams (etc) meet the criteria?*
- *If they meet the criteria then it is probably a good idea to evaluate before taking action so begin the evaluation process right away.*
- *If they don't meet the criteria then reflect on what stops you taking action and what is the most simple and obvious thing to do to make a start right away?*

- *Finally, reflect on this experiment and see what you notice: What did you notice about your must look first list? What did you notice when you ran your hopes, dreams and actions list through that criteria? What patterns do you notice here? How do you potentially confuse real fear and social anxiety? What could be a simple practice to short-circuit your usual habits?*

It is impossible to get this experiment wrong – just be curious as to what you notice.

This experiment is a helpful way of making the distinction between where genuine, instinctive fear prevents us from springing to action as opposed to our own limiting beliefs and social anxieties. Through continually reflecting and asking ourselves these questions, we can begin to use our lizard brain in a way where we allow it to fulfil its essential, instinctive, survival role but also train it to allow us more space for risk, experimentation and learning that is essential to nurturing our creative spirit.

Relationships - The Mammalian Brain (the limbic system)

Human beings are essentially herd animals and relationships are of utmost importance to us. We are highly dependent on others for our own survival, be that for love, security, reproduction, shelter or those who supply us with food in the form of anything  from pre-prepared ready meals to seeds to grow our own. (Even those who have had specialist training to survive in the wild begin to be adversely altered without contact with other human beings over an extended period time.) The prime directive of our mammalian brain is to preserve the relationships that nourish our basic needs, which is something that serves us well and not something we'd want to give up. However, the complex process of relating that human beings engage in on a daily basis is as much of a constraint as an enabler when it comes to creativity. The confused social anxiety arising from our lizard brain is amplified by our mammalian brain and results in a strong desire to limit any action that may damage important relationships and result in us being rejected by the herd. In a similar way that the fear function of the lizard brain inhibits our creativity, the mammalian brain's strong need to preserve relationships can seriously stifle our creative spirit.

Two of the major factors that influence the emphasis the mammalian brain puts on particular relationships are power and identity. Social Constructionists, such as George Mead[3] and Kenneth Gergen[4], suggest that our identity isn't a static thing that we are born with and stays with us for our entire lives but something that is continuously negotiated moment-by-moment in relation to others. Mead came up with the idea of what he called an on-going "*I-me*" dialect which I understand to mean that, at any point in time, my sense of who I am is a combination of my own perception of myself plus other's perception of me. Where there is a mutual overlap in perception then my identity is confirmed and my sense of self is validated. However, where there is a mismatch then my identity is challenged and I may feel awkward, misunderstood, angry or confused and need a period of reflection to alter or re-establish my sense of self. If I don't do this I begin to develop all sorts of psychological difficulties.

Power is a natural outcome of the process of relating and is an unavoidable part of being a sentient being - there is always a subtle dance of dominance and submission at some level in every interaction, even in highly symbiotic relationships. I find the term *status* a more helpful one than *power* as it suggests that these dynamics are not something we *have* but something we *do.* Status is essentially a choice about how we perceive others and ourselves in relation to each other (albeit a choice that may be unconsciously, socially or politically suppressed). As individuals, we don't have any particular power, we are simply participating in an on-going process of *statusing* with each other, a subtle dance of ever shifting patterns of dominance and submission based on our moment by moment needs. If we choose to no longer act into the socially established status patterns then the power dynamic is challenged and no longer exists in the same form. This can be observed in a variety of scenarios, from a leader who has a hierarchical position in an organisation but has no influence over his subordinates, right through to social movements, such as the Arab Spring of 2011, where whole communities chose to no longer act into the dominant power patterns that had been established. This dynamic gets even more complicated when we consider the combined impact of power and identity on our way of being - if somebody we perceive as having power over us challenges our identity it tends to have a far greater impact on us than somebody who we perceive as having less power.

Whilst patterns of power and identity permeate every part of our lives, they are particularly pronounced where social order is more highly structured and formalised and a tradition of dominance and submission has been established. With this in mind, it should come as no surprise that the prime relational directives of the mammalian brain are amplified and even more creatively inhibiting in the corporate world where hierarchy, role and rules are so heavily formalised. (To be clear, these patterns occur in *all* organisations but may be more or less pronounced dependant on the degree of formal hierarchy and the culture that has emerged around it. Gore Associates, for example, have no formal organisational hierarchy but even here subtle dances of status will still occur moment by moment as people interact and individual needs are negotiated.)

So, even if I managed to tame my lizard brain's fear of my own creative self, why would I then risk the prime relational directives of my mammalian brain by telling somebody about a wildly creative idea that they may think it is stupid? Why would I risk trying something new and innovative when there is the possibility that my boss or peers might think I'm incompetent if I screw it up? Why would I be overt about my own process of dreaming and imagining when I might risk getting cast out of the Serious Strategy Team as a tree hugging fruitcake? Often it is the case that we get into the habit of self-censoring and freezing our creative spirit because we are scared it will damage or irreversibly alter the relationships we are so reliant on. In a similar way to learning to work with the lizard brain, it is key we start to find some fruitful middle ground between maintaining the prime directives of the mammalian brain whilst liberating our creative spirit.

Experiment: Relational Self-Censoring

- On a piece of paper list all of the people you interact with on a regular basis: work, boss, colleagues, clients, family, friends, online interactions (etc). As many as possible.
- Imagine you wake up in the middle of the night with a wild idea. Something that is incredibly exciting that you feel could change the world but you've no idea of how you would make it work or whether it is in fact feasible. You may already have such an idea but if you don't it doesn't matter – it is the feeling that this idea creates that is most important.
- Draw a four box grid with "My comfort level" Lower/Higher on one axis and "Degree of dependence" Lower/Higher on the other.
- Look at your list of people and think about how dependent you are on maintaining that relationship and comfortable you would feel about telling them your idea (real or imagined). Place the name of each person in the relevant box on the grid.
- Reflect on the experience of this experiment: What do you notice about your grid? How did it feel when considering different people? How did it feel to complete the grid? What patterns or themes do you notice on the completed grid? How did you feel as you placed each person on it? Do different categories of people fall into different places?

It is impossible to get this experiment wrong – just be curious as to what you notice.

This experiment can help us to tease out what types of relationships either inhibit or enhance our creative spirit and, through becoming more aware of where these patterns occur, we can start to become more choiceful about whether we want to comply with or challenge our perceptions.

Logic - The Human Brain (the neocortex)

Wherever you are reading this, if you were to stand up and point, anywhere, randomly, people who were paying attention would likely look towards where you were pointing. However, if there were any animals in the vicinity they would, if they were interested, look at your pointing hand as opposed to the direction in which you were pointing. This  experiment (I hope you tried it!) demonstrates just one way in which the brain of human beings is wired differently to animals due to the presence of a unique third brain. All animals have a lizard brain of sorts that is programmed for survival. Many have a mammalian herding brain and a smaller neocortex but only we human beings have the oversized neocortex that I'm affectionately referring to as the human brain. Besides getting us to look at things and not somebody's pointing finger, our neocortex enables many uniquely human functions including language, sensory perception, motor commands and, most relevant when it comes to creativity, conscious thought and choiceful intention.

However, over time (and likely as a hangover from the dominant philosophies and mechanistic thinking that arose during the Industrial Revolution) we have biased our human brain to focus on logic and deductive reasoning – the ability to break anything down to its component parts, label and explain it! This has led to an unspoken mantra in modern society and business that if something cannot be logically explained, justified or measured then it does not exist! (I'm reminded of the naïve and controlling Kangaroo in the Dr Seuss Book

"Horton hears a Who"[5], who teaches the children that *"If you can't see, hear or feel something then it doesn't exist."*)

Whilst our logical and deductive abilities have proven invaluable in our on-going endeavours as a species, they also play a major role in stifling our creativity, or at least ensuring that we keep it bottled up and buried deep within us. As referenced in Chapter 1, this phenomenon is amplified as we move from childhood, through adolescence and into adulthood and the deductive, logical patterns of thinking become more dominant, habitual and unconscious.

The dominance of logical, deductive thought is the third major factor that inhibits our creative spirit as it has the power to crush the often wild green shoots of our imagination before they have a chance to blossom into something special. The *Creative Thought vs. Logical Death* table on the next page shows a number of ways in which our well-developed human logic has become very adept at killing novel thoughts offered up by our creative spirit with a simple/swift blow. That fatal blow may be self-inflicted or dealt through the words of others who are also being protected by their human brain's logical prime directives.

There are no doubt many more ways in which ideas are sentenced to *Logical Death,* these were simply some that I can remember telling myself or others telling me over the years. The last one on the list  is one I remember very well indeed. On 3rd September 2012, as I walked from the south to the north side of Hungerford Bridge in London my mind was wandering. I was curious as to what experiment I could come up with that would teach me something about the human creative spirit. Out of nowhere I found myself coming up with *The Giraffe Project*. I would ask 100 random people to draw a picture of a giraffe and then ask them questions about their thoughts and feelings having done it. I knew that if I procrastinated that I would talk myself out of it so I set about creating a giraffe experiment pack and dropped over 100 envelopes in the post.

Creative Thought	Logical Death (a handful of examples)
"I've an idea.....I wonder what would happen if..."	"That's a ridiculous idea!" (i.e. it sounds so different to what has already been proven to work that I cannot entertain the thought of it having any benefit.)
	"OK, how will you make it work?" (i.e. unless you can come up with a plan of making it a reality there is no point in even coming up with it.)
	"That's been done before" (i.e. there is no point in repeating something that has already been proven a failure or a success by others. The past = the future.)
	"You are stupid." (i.e. this idea is beyond my comprehension so logically it isn't me but you that is at fault here.)
	"OK, you'll never convince (person x, y) that this is a good idea." (i.e. this idea scares me but even if I did get it you would never convince others, so don't bother!)
	"What is the return on investment for this?" (i.e. something is only worth starting if we know we are guaranteed to end up better off.)
	"What do you hope to achieve from this? How will you measure success?" (i.e. a good idea is only worth having if you have worked out what you want to get from it and know how you will know you've got it!)

Over the next six months more and more beautiful, unique creations dropped through my door, every one of them different and every one of them giving some insight into the self-limiting beliefs, assumptions and instinctive responses of the individual. The insights from the *Giraffe Project* ended up helping me to distil the chapters and focus areas of this book as well as creating a wonderful gallery of animals drawn by people aged five to 95. (You can view them at www.thegiraffeproject.com). It was a wonderfully enriching, insightful and fun experiment to undertake and it seemed to make everyone who took part smile and bring a little playfulness into their lives irrelevant of what they thought of their picture.

However, throughout the entire project, from day one, right up until the last giraffe arrived, the idea was continually subjected to attacks of logic. Almost everyone I mentioned it to asked me *"What do you hope to achieve?"*, *"What are you trying to prove?"* or *"What does success look like?"* Whether they were intending to or not, these questions activated my logical brain and I almost talked myself out of continuing as I didn't have an answer and started to feel a bit stupid. When I thought of having to have an answer to these questions I felt the magic and energy I had for the project draining away. I was simply wondering what would happen if I asked a 100 people to draw a giraffe and hadn't thought it through any further than that! Thankfully I managed to occupy my logical brain with other things such as finance spread sheets and forecasts for long enough to complete the experiment and I am still enjoying the magic that the *Giraffe Project* brought to the world. I learnt from this experience the power *Logical Death* has to kill potential creative thought and wanton experimentation and experienced the personal resilience required to overcome it. I also learnt that if you do not have a plan for where an experiment *should* go – anywhere it goes is just wonderful!

You may be noticing a pattern emerging across these three brains. Each one simultaneously enables us whilst it constrains us. Each prime directive serves us well and, at the same time, stifles our creative spirit. As with the lizard and the mammalian brain, the way to start working with the human brain is to begin to increase our awareness of a more fruitful and less stifling middle ground, where the satisfaction of both needs is better balanced.

Experiment: Logical Death vs. Creative Life

Part I   *Come up with as many reasons as you can for why the following ideas are impractical, stupid, illogical or simply bad. You cannot have too many reasons so take great delight in destroying and crushing these ideas.*

- *A saucepan that is made of newspaper.*
- *A theme park for dogs and cats.*
- *An underwater nursery school/kindergarten.*
- *A new type of coffee that is guaranteed to make you violently ill for exactly one hour.*
- *An airplane seat that has a 0.1% chance of being ejected during a flight.*
- *An 'everything's OK' alarm that emits a high-pitched shriek every 10 seconds as long as everything is OK. (I must credit Homer Simpson for this one!)*

Part II   *Below is a list of words. Pick two at random, don't think about it, maybe just point randomly at the page or get somebody else to pick two. The instant you have picked two come up with a new object, product or service and write it down. For example: CAR + SEAGULL = a car that has anti-seagull poo paint on it or ELECTRIC + SHIRT = a shirt that has an electrical current passing through it that stops people getting too close to you on a crowded train. The key is to do it as quickly as possible with minimal pre-thought or planning. Are these good ideas? It doesn't matter! The key is to come up with them and write them down as quick as possible without pre-thought or logical filtering. Carry on for as long as you like but come up with at least five or six ideas.*

CAR, SEAGUL, COFFEE, SEWER, POPE, TAIL, SUIT, BUS, CASH POINT, UMBRELLA, CUPBOARD, SWEETS, CAKE, THE QUEEN, ELECTRIC, PLANT, CHILDREN, THERAPY, COMPUTER, BOOK, DUCK, SMILE, PRIVATE, UNDERWEAR, HOLIDAY, HAUNTED, DRUGS, NAPKIN, TABLE, CHAIR, TAXI, SHIRT, EARRINGS, SONG, LIGHT, DOCTOR, POLITICIAN, CIGARETTE, SMOKING, MEXICAN, SUBMARINE, SQUIRREL, MUMMY, BADGER, MOUNTAIN, CULTURE, MONEY, CLOUD, SUNSHINE, VOLCANO, ILLUSION, MUD, MIRROR, HOSPITAL, LEG, DINOSAUR.

Making friends with Fear, Relationship and Logic

Fear, Relationships and Logic are three major barriers that stifle our creative spirit but, at the same time, also serve us well. In order to begin to release and nurture our natural creativity we must start to become deeply curious about our habits and beliefs and, in doing so, start to experiment with  teasing out a more symbiotic middle ground where our survival is not threatened *and* our creative spirit can flourish. A middle ground where we mitigate only the most life threatening risks whilst simultaneously allowing adventure to unfold and possibly take us by surprise. A middle ground that we might think of as a place of "*Safe Uncertainty*"[6]. (This is a term coined by therapist Barry Mason that is explored further in Chapter 5)

The intent of my simplistic description of the human condition is to give hope that recovering more of our creative selves doesn't require us to undertake a PhD in creativity, become a proficient artist or to go and live in a creative commune for 10 years but for us simply to become more self-aware and recover some long-lost choices. However, it is also important not to confuse simple with easy and to remember that this is a process of letting go of old stuff more than it is of learning new stuff. This process is more or less difficult dependent on one's age, background, schooling, professional training, environment (etc) as the habits and norms that inhibit us are likely to have become more unconscious and more deeply ingrained over time and in certain contexts. Before we can begin our Creative Adventures we need to find ways of overcoming the barriers of fear, relationships and logic by becoming more aware of when and where they stifle us. We are effectively re-wiring ourselves here and, as the old saying goes, *neurons that fire together, wire together,* so continual practice is key.

Re-wiring for Adventure			
Instinctive barrier to creativity	Positive traits for survival	Negative impact on creativity	Fruitful middle ground (Safe Uncertainty)
FEAR *Driven by prime directives of lizard brain.*	Safety through triggering of our fight or flight response. Ensures we eat, do not die and are able to reproduce.	Fight-or-flight kicks in when survival is not threatened and closes down our peripheral awareness and creative potential as we retreat to 'safe certainty'	A greater awareness of the distinction between real fear and social anxiety.
RELATIONSHIPS *Driven by prime directives of mammalian brain.*	Fulfils our need for connectivity, love, togetherness, and symbiosis.	Dramatic self-censoring of instinctive, spontaneous and creative thought in order to preserve relationships.	A greater awareness of where one's real or perceived patterns of identity and power cause over censoring.
LOGIC *Driven by prime directives of human brain.*	A 'higher' function of the human condition that allows us to problem solve, plan, strategise and evaluate.	Habitual "*instant death sentence*" for non-linear, non-logical, unproven creative ideas before they have chance to grow.	Exercise and strengthen the curious, experimental and spontaneous "*what would happen if?*" muscle to recover choice as to whether logic is helpful or not.

The good news is that you can begin your Creative Adventure immediately as no further materials or resources are needed. You require nothing other than a curious mind and a deep interest in yourself and the present moment. In fact......All You Need is NOW!

Chapter 2 References

1   Learnfest 2013 A wonderful event dubbed "The Glastonbury of Learning" run by Impact International

2   Gordon MacKenzie (1996) "*Orbiting the Giant Hairball: A Corporate Fool's Guide to Surviving with Grace.*" New York: Penguin Group

3   George Meade (1932) "*The Philosophy of the Present.*" Chicago: Open Court Pub.

4   Kenneth Gergen (1999) *An Invitation to Social Construction.* 2nd edn, London: Sage

5   Dr Seuss (1954) "*Horton Hears a Who.*" Random House Children's Books

6   Barry Mason (1993) "*Towards Positions of Safe Uncertainty*" in *Human Systems: The Journal of Systemic Consultation & Management Vol 4*

Chapter 3 All You Need is NOW!

"When you cut into the present, the future leaks out."
William S Burroughs (1914-1997)

I am aware this chapter might be a bit heavier than the rest. That is because it looks to explore a subject that is rather profound and elusive – the concept of time itself! However, reflecting on one's own perceptions of time and how we can unleash our creative spirit through  paying more attention to the present moment is a vital part of embarking on a Creative Adventure, so I believe the potential heaviness will be worth it in the end!

It seems to me that, despite the plethora of books on change management/self-help and armies of consultants and coaches selling the latest model of organisational or personal transformation, there are only two rules about change that appear to be true: 1) You can only change yourself and 2) You can only change the present moment. These two rules lie at the heart of discovering or reviving our creative spirit. This is good news as it means that, rather than scouring the four corners of the world to find answers, we actually have everything we need within us in the present moment to kick start our own Creative Adventures. In the same way that the poet William Blake suggests that a curious mind can *"see the world in a grain of sand"*[1], all of the cues and clues we need to unleash a more creative version of ourselves are encapsulated in every moment of our being - we just need to learn how to become more aware of and curious about our lived experience and become a kind-of creative auto-anthropologist!

The Gestalt psychologist Arnold Beisser conceived of what he called the *"Paradoxical Theory of Change"*[2] which he eloquently describes as *"Change occurs when one becomes more of what he is, not when he tries to become more of what he is not"*. Basically what Beisser is suggesting is that we get more change through paying greater attention to who we already are, as opposed to aspiring to become something we are not. This may sound confusing and contrary to a lot of the things we have been taught but that's why he labelled it as paradoxical!

Whilst it isn't necessarily easy to get one's head intellectually around Beisser's theory, it is quite simple to begin to develop an understanding through practice. By mentally and physically slowing down, focussing all of our attention on ourselves and becoming deeply curious about our thoughts, feelings, sensations, emotions and bodily reactions we become more aware of how we may stifle or liberate our creative spirit moment by moment. Having done this, we can then become even more curious about the things we've noticed, study them in detail, chew them over, work out what needs they are serving within us and whether those needs are conscious or unconscious, helpful or unhelpful and whether they unintentionally sabotage our creativity or enhance it.

My friend and colleague at On Your Feet (www.oyf.com), Robert Poynton, has a beautifully simple model that has many uses and I find particularly helpful as an aid to help us mine the present moment for clues about our unconscious habits, beliefs and assumptions.

Rob's model, that can be found in his books "*Everything's an Offer*"[3] and "*Do: Improvise*"[4] is *Let Go, Notice More and Use Everything.*

Experiment: Mining the present moment for minerals of creativity

Part I   As best you can, try to **Let go** of any thoughts and fantasies about the future and any memories of the past. Focus all of your attention on the experience of now. Be as precise as possible about this - even something 10 seconds ago or 10 seconds ahead is not the present moment. Gradually and gently usher your attention away from fantasies or memories until you feel that you are as focussed as you can be on now.

Part II   Allow yourself to begin to **Notice More** about how you are in the present moment. Become intensely curious about the entirety of your current experience. What are you thinking about? Where do your thoughts keep wanting to wander to? What are you feeling? What emotions or bodily sensations do you notice? How is your breathing? Where in your body is your attention? What happens if you slowly move your attention to different parts? What sense do your toes make of now? How about your small intestine? What can you smell, taste, hear, touch or see? Don't worry about having to name or label your observations or rationalise them if you cannot find the words. You don't have to present your noticing to anyone else, you simply need to notice how you are and acknowledge it.

This experiment is about trying to see the world in a grain of sand – to notice the entirety of our life experience enfolded in a moment in time.   As Beisser suggests, through paying greater attention to these moments and noticing how they are littered with our conscious and unconscious habits, we begin to change by simply becoming more aware of who we already are.   This experiment is simple but not easy.   It gets easier with practice but, ironically, the moment it becomes effortless is the moment we realise we're not doing it right as we are avoiding the difficult and interesting things embedded deep in the next layer of our awareness.

I have become fascinated by the idea that all of the historical choices I have made and lessons I have learnt about my own creativity during my life influence the conscious and unconscious choices I make in the present moment.   To learn more about these ideas I decided to devote my MSc dissertation back in 2011 to inquire further.   My final paper ended up being 21,500 words inspired by becoming deeply curious about 150 seconds of my life. Through the use of audio and video recordings and journal entries, I mined each moment of these 150 seconds to see what clues about my own creativity I could surface and was fascinated by the new questions that handful of seconds uncovered – questions I am still exploring and unpacking many years on that have significantly influenced this book. I learnt from this experience that, rather than seek answers from experts, academics or literature all we really need to do to develop a greater understanding of our creative abilities is to take our moment by moment experience seriously and begin to place a greater value in the power of *now*!

The Architecture of NOW

In his book *"The Present Moment"*[5] Daniel Stern suggests that *now* is made up of three overlapping moments: *"A present-of-the-present moment, a past-of-the-present-moment and a future-of-*  *the-present-moment."* Simply put, he suggests that our immediate and retained past (i.e. a moment ago and historical) and our anticipated or imagined future all influence our meaning making in the present. Whilst Stern's suggestion is essentially only a convenient model to illustrate something far more complex, it does help us understand how all significant memories of the past and fantasies of the future are enfolded somewhere in the moment that you find yourself reading this sentence. Some of these memories and fantasies are more conscious than others. Sometimes they become more figural and front-of-mind, depending on the context and circumstances that we find ourselves in. However conscious or unconscious they are, they have an influence on the choices we make at any particular moment and play a role in helping or hindering our creative spirit.

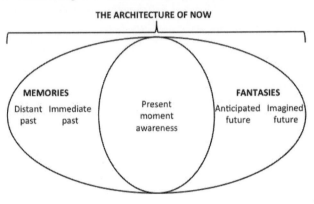

THE ARCHITECTURE OF NOW

MEMORIES

Distant past   Immediate past

Present moment awareness

FANTASIES

Anticipated future   Imagined future

During my dissertation research I uncovered a number of significant events from the past, introjected rules about how I should be and fantasies about the future that I found inhibited my spontaneous creativity from emerging in the moment. Many of these insights were to do with my devaluing of these skills as I grew up, perceptions about power and status that caused me to self-censor, habitual transference onto particular types of people (in particular older men in positions of authority) as well as rules about the separation between work and play and what it meant to be a professional in the corporate world. I also realised that I projected these memories of the past onto anticipated future experiences, unconsciously cutting and pasting self-limiting beliefs onto something that had not yet happened. I noticed that all of this caused me to work to an idealised script of how I should be as opposed to truly being my spontaneous self and working live in-the-moment. Having become more aware of how perceptions of the past and future impacted on my here-and-now actions I began to experiment by challenging my habits in ever-so subtle ways and gradually began to recover more choice about how much of my creative self I would bring into the present moment. I found this incredibly challenging but also deeply liberating. However, I was left with another question – how long is this moment called *now* and how significant is its length in this process of sense making? This question left me with a brain ache akin to eating ice cream too quickly so I decided to delve even deeper into my beliefs and assumptions about the overall concept of time.

A kairos vs chronos perspective of time

Time, as we commonly refer to it, is an invention of the human mind. It is a social construction - something that, over many years, we have agreed is a good idea as a way of orientating ourselves to the movements of the solar system and making sure we get to our next meeting on time. This social construction is so  predominant in our lives that it is somewhat disturbing to realise that essentially, time as we know it, doesn't really exist. Our modern perception of time is known as *chronos* time or what we commonly call *clock time* – the on-going progression of seconds, minutes and hours that tick away on our watches, clocks and electronic systems all over the world. Daniel Stern argues that, if *chronos* time were real then the moment of *now* would be *"so fleeting and irrecoverable"* that we would never be able to dwell in it long enough to make meaning of our experience. We would rapidly move on from one discreet micro-experience to another. If *chronos* were literally true we would experience our lives like an extreme goldfish whose awareness of the past and the future extends to +/- one second! The Greek concept of *kairos* is an alternative perspective of time. Instead of being defined by seconds, minutes and hours, *kairos* time is simply a passing moment of consciousness in which something happens that allows us to make new meaning of our experience.

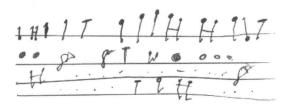

This can initially be a confusing concept so it can be helpful to think that we experience a moment of *kairos* in a similar way to how we experience a musical phrase as a whole and not a sequence of individual and unrelated notes. From his research Stern suggests that a period of anywhere between two to eight seconds appears to be enough *chronos* to allow a moment of *kairos* to occur and calls these events "*present moments*" - episodes of consciousness that exist between periods of unconscious awareness, the sum of which forms the basis of our on-going perception. Put simply, I like to think of *chronos* being a concept of time informed by clocks and *kairos* being a concept of time informed by meaning.

I often wonder what the world would be like if we abandoned *chronos* time! What would happen if we began to run our lives and our organisations based on a philosophy of *kairos* time? What would happen to our working days, how would we interact, what would our meetings look and feel like?

Instead of a *chronos*-bound start and end point to each agenda item, what if we just interacted for as long as was required for new collective meaning to emerge? Some agenda items might take 10 times as long, whilst others may only take seconds. What would happen if we let go of the meeting discipline of *time keeping* in favour of *meaning making* – the discipline of being overt with one's own clarity, confusion and learning whilst checking in with others as to where collective meaning had been made or was lacking. What if our entire workday was organised around these *kairos* principles and our diaries, locations and interactions were completely governed by what meaning needed to be made at any particular moment in order to propel our business into the future? Most relevant for this book is the question whether a more *kairos* informed culture would enable us more space to discover and play with our creative spirit?

I'm not suggesting that *kairos* is an overall better philosophy of time than *chronos*, however I admit to believing that it is an overall more helpful concept for allowing creativity to emerge. I am intrigued as to what would happen if we were to experiment by adjusting this bias and allowing our individual and collective creative needs to govern how we interact rather than a overly time-bound structure. I often say to groups who are trying to innovate but appear rather too addicted to their pre-ordained meeting structures *"Are you managing your*

agenda or is your agenda managing you?" or *"Are you trying to do it quickly or do it properly?"* or I suggest that *"There is no breathing space in this meeting for possibility, novelty or creativity to emerge".* Daniel Stern asks a more fundamental question *"How can we pry open chronos to create a present long enough to accommodate kairos?"* The relevant question for those wanting to embark on a Creative Adventure is *"How much does our dominant perception of chronos time inhibit moments of creative kairos?"*

So what for creativity?

If we can spend some time getting our head around the concept of *kairos* time, the limitations of a purely *chronos* perspective and become more aware of how the past and future are all enfolded into the present, we begin to realise that everything we need to better understand and unleash our creative spirit is right here and right now. All of our historical/future choices about our own creativity are active and embedded in the present moment and keep our creative spirit in check. However exciting this is, if we were to become deeply curious about literally *everything* in *every* moment our heads would metaphorically explode with sensory and information overload. It is therefore helpful to have a rough frame for our curiosity. A lens to help us notice more of what is helpful to us in our creative quest. Not a set of criteria or actions that are unhelpfully narrow or overly logical but some simple navigation aids that give us just enough guidance to make sense of our experiences and allow us to step boldly into the unknown.

Through on-going experimentation and research into the creative barriers of *Fear, Relationships and Logic* (See

Chapter 2) I noticed that a number of major themes kept cropping up – recurring, deeply embedded habits, norms and beliefs that seemingly keep our creativity in check. Over time and through learning from others in the creative field, I have synthesised these observations into six simple creative practices. I regularly use these practices to help nurture and develop my own creative spirit and have blended them into my creativity, innovation and coaching work in the corporate world. They are a very simple and powerful lens to help make sense of our lived experience of *now* and enable us to become more aware of the unconscious habits and beliefs that keep our creative spirit suppressed.

Part II of this book describes these six creative practices in detail.

Chapter 3 References

1 William Blake (1863) *"Auguries of Innocence"*

2 Arnold Beisser (1970) *"The Paradoxical Theory of Change"* in J.Fagan and L.L. Shepard (eds) *Gestalt Therapy Now.* New York: Science and Behaviour Books

3 Robert Poynton (2008) *"Everything's an Offer: How to do More with Less."* Portland: On Your Feet

4 "Robert Poynton (2013) *"Do Improvise: Less Push. More Pause. Better Results. A New Approach to Work (and Life)"* Do Books

5 Daniel Stern (2004) *"The Present Moment - In Psychotherapy and everyday life."* New York:W.W.Norton & Co.

PART TWO

CREATIVE PRACTICES

Chapter 4 Mad, Bad and Wrong
Letting go of our need to be perpetually seen as sane, good and right

Hatter: *"Have I gone mad?"*
Alice: *"I'm afraid so. You're entirely bonkers. But I'll tell you a secret. All the best people are!"*

Alice in Wonderland

In a coffee shop recently I was watching the breakfast television news whilst I waited for my drink. On it was a story about an investigation into UK supermarkets misleading consumers by  advertising big discounts on products that had previously been artificially inflated in price. The programme flicked from a recorded piece out on the street to the news anchor in the studio. He looked at the camera and said, with a tone intended to further inflame the scandalous nature of the story, *"This is an outrage. These supermarkets make millions and nobody is regulating this sort of thing. The regulations we've got in place are not enough."* He then turned to a studio guest, presumably some sort of expert in either politics or supermarkets and said *"We need something drastically different here. What can we do to send a message once and for all that this is not acceptable?"* The guest turned to him, paused and said *"Well, I've got an idea I call The Village Stocks. Any supermarket found guilty of this, no matter how big or small, is required to shut for one minute as an act of public humiliation and to show that this practice will not be tolerated."* The presenter looked at his guest as if she had just turned into some sort of crazed escaped lunatic. *"That is the most preposterous idea I have ever heard. I'm sorry, in all my years of broadcasting that is the most ridiculous response to a question ever!"* He turned to another studio guest who hadn't yet spoken. She weighed in to add *"How on earth would you make that work? Imagine the logistical nightmare it would cause, let alone the inconvenience for shoppers."* As I left the coffee shop I witnessed the last few moments as a newly hatched imaginative, creative idea, full of possibility and opportunity, suffered a very brutal and very public execution.

The internal PR Department

My six year-old daughter is my creative mentor and Chief of Imagination at Can Scorpions Smoke Change and Creativity Ltd. Often when I'm designing a new piece of work I will ask her to help me with it, give me ideas and advise me on how to make it a creative experience for  others. She always comes up with something that is beautifully simple, often a little out-there and it shakes up my thinking and disturbs any stale patterns of habitual thought that I may be slipping into. Recently she has been helping me with my *Imagination to Innovation* workshops which are experimental and experiential sessions that strip the process of innovation right back to the simple, but not easy, childlike process of dreaming and imagining in front of others. For each client, I ask my mentor if she could invent something that would make the organisation's life easier. I then share the invention with the participants to demonstrate the type of unbounded concept generation we are looking to achieve during the workshop.

 For example, when working recently with a digital telecoms company, she came up with the *"Lu Lu Rainbow Phone."* It is a wildly colourful phone that has arms and legs and, not only dials the people you tell it to, it also has the conversation with them on your behalf! In addition to this, the phone can call and talk with other electronic household items such as toasters and washing machines and has a special battery that lasts 1,000 years. Now, is that a life-changing invention? Is it even technologically possible? Who knows? It could be if the ideas were developed further and avoided being sentenced to *Logical Death* (See Chapter 2) like the supermarket village stocks idea was. Whilst I love the innovative and out-there ideas my daughter comes up with, the thing that interests me most is the thought process by which she comes up with them. It seems relatively simple: I tell her who my client is, she appears to pause ever so briefly and then say the first thing that comes into her head. She then draws it and adds spontaneous detail as she draws, boldly and without any fear of whether the idea is good enough or if it is feasible to turn into a reality. This seems to be a process that most children under eight are able to immediately engage in – a process of tapping into a flowing, improvised stream of creativity.

In his book *"Improvisation: Its nature and in practice"*[1] Derek Bailey tells a story of interviewing Jazz saxophonist Steve Lacy. *"I took out my pocket tape recorder and asked him to describe in fifteen seconds the difference between composition and improvisation. He answered: 'In fifteen seconds the difference between composition and*

improvisation is that, in composition you have all the time you want to decide what to say in fifteen seconds, while in improvisation you have fifteen seconds!"' The description of the latter seems to be the world in which young children perpetually inhabit – spontaneously acting into a moment without pre-thought or self-censoring.

Theatre Director Keith Johnstone once said that anybody can improvise and be creative if they are able to get over their fear of being perceived as mad, bad or wrong by others. The fear that others may think we are insane, unethical, uncaring, irresponsible or incorrect seems to be one of the biggest factors in keeping our creative geniuses deeply frozen. As adults, it is almost as if each of us have our own internal personal PR department, located somewhere between our brain and our body, that vets our spontaneous, creative ideas to see if they could be perceived as mad, bad or wrong by others and damage our relationships or threaten our survival. Young children are yet to develop these habits to the extent that us adults have.

As I reflect on my own life, I can start to see how this internal PR department became so powerful and how my own fears of being perceived as mad, bad or wrong grew as I did and slowly suffocated my creative spirit. I can recall vividly times when I got answers spectacularly wrong at school. In a history lesson, aged 11 or so, I remember the teacher asking the class *"Who knows what the holocaust was?"* From out of nowhere the obvious answer popped into my head, I waved my hand in the air and proudly answered *"The end of the world!"* to the laughter of my peers and the disapproving scowl of my teacher who didn't even acknowledge my effort and went elsewhere to get the right answer. (On reflection it seems that I had got the words apocalypse and holocaust mixed up, although I do see *some* validity in my answer now having a better understanding of the horrors of the latter.)

As I bring to mind my maths homework it still triggers the same hot-brain-overload feeling today that it did back then. Maths was never a strength of mine and I struggled with it throughout my entire time at school. This was made worse as I seemed to be surrounded by many well intentioned people who were quick to point out where I'd got it wrong, believing that this would help me get it right. In the end I just didn't bother trying for fear of being told I was wrong. My early experiences of work also had a negative impact on my spontaneous self-confidence. One of my first jobs was in a factory and I vividly remember an engineer showing my manager pictures of a machine they were going to install. It seemed obvious to me that the machine was too big to fit through the doors into the room where it was to be installed. I voiced my concerns but the two of them responded by tutting and suggested that, as a lowly 18 year-old production operator, I was crazy to ask such a question – lots of complicated drawings and calculations had been done by people better qualified than me. I decided they must be right and didn't pursue my question any further. (I found out years later when telling this tale to an ex-colleague of mine that the machine *didn't* fit through the doors and a wall had to be removed which put the project way over budget!)

These are just a handful of many, seemingly insignificant, life events that led to a habit of denying my creativity and self-censoring my spontaneous thought in order to mitigate being perceived as mad, bad or wrong – the memories of the embarrassment and stigma I felt at the time becoming invisibly embedded in the present moment. Over time, these habits became more and more unconscious to the point where I simply no longer felt creative. Since then I have coached many others who describe a similar damping experience. It seems the mad, bad and wrong logic we use here is well intentioned but problematic – it is better to sacrifice creativity and spontaneity than risk loss of reputation or experience humiliation. Early on in life this probably serves us very well as it helps us find the boundaries of what is ethical, moral and legal in modern society. However, over time, the logic expands exponentially and can become a barrier to leading a more adventurous and exciting life with these experiences of the past inhibiting ourselves in the present.

Experiment: Origins of Mad, Bad and Wrong

- *Draw a venn diagram with three overlapping circles. Label each circle MAD, BAD and WRONG.*
- *Sit still for a moment, try to empty your mind and simply become more aware of your body and senses.*
- *Bring to mind as many times as you can when you can recall feeling that you were perceived as mad by others: having an idea that others thought was stupid or crazy or a time when you did something that others regarded as mad. Write it down in the MAD circle. (Note: it only needs to make sense to you so feel free to abbreviate to single words or a symbol.)*
- *Then bring to mind as many times as you can when you can recall being perceived as bad by others: a time where something you did either intentionally or unintentionally caused others to think that your actions were inconsiderate, cruel or unappreciative of a person, a situation or a context. Write it down in the BAD circle. (Note: these examples can be as big or as little as you like – treat nothing as insignificant.)*
- *Finally, bring to mind as many times as you can when you recall being perceived as wrong by others: doing something that wasn't right, giving a wrong answer, being overtly incorrect, taking a wrong direction or giving bad advice. Write it down in the WRONG circle.*

- Reflect on your diagram: What do you notice? Are there any patterns? Do you notice that some events feel more powerful than others? Do any other events come to mind? How easy was it to think of these events? What might have made this experiment easy/difficult?
- Reflect on where you feel you inhibit your creativity in the present: How much do you feel these events affect your spontaneous creative choices? Where in your life or your work do you feel that you self-censor in order to mitigate from others seeing you as mad, bad or wrong?

It is impossible to get this experiment wrong – just be curious as to what you notice.

Embracing Mad, Bad and Wrong

Those who are able to make friends with and tame their fear of being perceived as mad, bad or wrong are better able to experiment, break new ground, innovate and breath new creative energy into every part of their lives no matter how big or small. One of my own passions is cooking and one of my favourite cookbooks is by a creative American  chef named Eric Gower. Gower spent many years living and working in Tokyo where he pioneered a new way of cooking that he calls *Breakaway*. The ethos of Breakaway is essentially to *"breath new life into old ingredients"* and give birth to some incredible new dishes. Eric's first book *"The Breakaway Japanese Kitchen"*[2] was written whilst he lived and worked in Tokyo and fuses traditional Japanese cuisine with Gower's imaginative *Breakaway* method. At the same time he also embarked on a mission to bring Matcha, an epicurean powdered Japanese tea normally reserved for tea ceremonies, to the masses as an alternative, healthy hot drink. I interviewed him in early 2013 as I was curious to find out what made him tick creatively and to get an idea of some of the mad, bad and wrong challenges I imagined he faced trying to innovate and experiment with the cuisine of a culture steeped in history and tradition. *"It upset people"* he told me, *"Inevitably somebody would stand up and say 'this is completely outrageous, you cannot desecrate Japanese cooking this way!'"* Gower's creative vision for Japanese cuisine caused him to be regularly labelled in public as being mad, bad and *very* wrong. Many of us would have become disheartened and found it easier to give up and concede our ambition rather than carry on and exacerbate the mad, bad and wrong label, so I asked him how he responded to such criticisms. *"I'd tell them, look, this is actually a labour of love, I'm actually trying to breath new life into these ingredients by thinking of them in ways you might not have."* It was his own passion and personal determination that gave Gower the resilience to continue in the face of adversity and what he told me next I found very inspiring. *"Some of my most vociferous disbelievers or critics often became zealous believers in Breakaway style because I'd somehow given them permission to do something they had been told their entire lives they couldn't do."*

We normally experience being perceived as mad bad and wrong because we are bumping up against and challenging the boundaries of tradition and habit – we stand out as being different to the norm. What Eric Gower managed to eventually achieve was only done through his ability to dampen his own fears as to how he was perceived because his personal mission was so important to him. Through doing this, not only did he create a new style of cooking, he also gave permission to others to allow themselves to be a little more mad, bad and wrong with their own – dissolving an imagined psychological and social boundary as to what was creatively possible.

A fear of being perceived as mad, bad or wrong by others stifles our creativity, our ability to dream, imagine and improvise and ultimately our ability to innovate and adapt to the things that life throws at us. This practice is about gently dampening this fear and letting go of a need to always be perceived as sane, good and right. This practice is about experimenting through placing a greater trust in our spontaneous instincts, thoughts and feelings far more than we normally allow ourselves to. It is about becoming more aware of how much of our fear is about what others may think about us and how much is about what we might think about ourselves. It is about working out where our internal PR department serves us well in terms of being able to live, thrive and relate as a human being whilst simultaneously getting more into the habit of *leaping and then looking*, (see Chapter 2) trusting that our gut instinct and little creative genius isn't going to steer us too wrong.

Experiment: The Goldilocks Zone of Mad, Bad and Wrong

The purpose of this experiment is to find our 'Goldilocks Zone' of mad, bad and wrong. A way of being that isn't too comfortable, nor too uncomfortable but just right.

- *Draw three concentric circles and label them as Too Comfortable, Just Right and Too Uncomfortable.*
- *Bring to mind something you want to try. You might think of something you've always wanted to do or something you've been procrastinating over. You might think about where you feel you are self-limiting or something you want to develop. The key is that it is something that will help propel your own Creative Adventure into the future.*

Summary: Mad, Bad and Wrong

Beginning to dampen our fear of being perceived as mad, bad or wrong is an essential, on-going practice to begin to unleash our creative spirit. However, we can only begin to make friends with  this fear by teasing it out from its hiding place and we can only do this through experimentation – putting ourselves in situations where we have genuine experiences of feeling mad, bad or wrong. Once we get comfortable with ever-so gently leaning into our discomfort, we begin to amaze ourselves at the wonderful insights and adventures that start to emerge in an almost effortlessly way. Adopting this practice doesn't necessarily mean that we are no longer perceived as mad, bad or wrong by others – it simply means that we care less if we are!

Mad, Bad and Wrong	
Let go	• The need to always be seen as sane, good and right. • The need to pass every spontaneous thought through your internal PR department. • Sentencing new-born ideas to a logical death.
Be more	• Trusting of your own spontaneous instincts. • Challenging of organisational, cultural, social and self-imposed boundaries as to what is acceptable or possible. • Mad, bad and wrong (little and often).
Experiment by	• Becoming more aware of self-censoring. • Finding your own Mad, Bad and Wrong *'Goldilocks Zone.'* • Testing to see if the response of others to what you perceive as Mad, Bad and Wrong is really as awful as you might imagine.

Chapter 4 References

1 Derek Bailey (1980) "Improvisation: Its Nature and in Practice" Ashbourne: Mooreland Publishing

2 Eric Gower (2003) "*The Breakaway Japanese Kitchen: Inspired New Tastes*" Tokyo:Kodasha International

Chapter 5   Say "Yes" (to the mess)
Letting go of habitually saying "no"

"The big question is whether you are going to be able to say a hearty yes to your adventure." Joseph Campbell (1904-1987)

In his book *"Yes man"*[1], English comedian Danny Wallace tells the story of the year he decided to say *"yes"* to literally everything! His friends had accused him of being boring and saying *"no"* far too much and the book is a biographical account of what  happened. He tells some incredible tales about doing things he never would have dreamed of doing in the past, meeting new people, visiting new places and meeting his future wife. However, he also got into massive debt, got into fights and ended up in some rather dangerous and sleazy locations. Danny learnt that, rather than saying *"yes"* to everything, the key was striking a better balance between *yes* and *no* and a realisation, as Keith Johnstone so eloquently puts it, that *"people who say no are rewarded with the safety they attain, whilst the people that say yes are rewarded with the adventures they have"*.[2]

The language of adventure

This practice is about experiencing what it is like to say *"yes"* more, getting a better understanding of how habitual it is for us to say *"no"* and to understand the difference between adventure and safety, tweaking the balance more towards the former. It is also about learning to love *the mess*. Things move on and change very quickly when you say *"yes"* more and *the mess* occurs when the amount of new experiences that we have overtakes our ability to make sense of them. When you say *"yes"* you go far fast and can find yourself in some unfamiliar places or states of mind before you know it – this is *the mess*. The mess is like a fog of confusion where we finds ourselves in a situation that is difficult to make sense of. I first heard the term *"Yes to the mess"*[3] from Frank Barrett, a Professor of Management and Organisation Behaviour and a talented Jazz musician who published a book of the same name in 2013. Barrett uses some of the lessons of his improvised Jazz experiences as a way of exploring change and leadership and talks of the importance of developing an ability to say *"yes"* whilst in the midst of the mess. Barrett describes the skills required to say *"yes"* to the mess as a Jazz musician, a leader or simply as a human being as an ability to *"Interpret vague cues, face unstructured tasks, process incomplete knowledge and take action anyway."* This description encapsulates what *saying "yes" to the mess* is all about.

Yes is the language of creativity and innovation because we are bypassing the internal censor who likes to be overly conservative and evaluate ideas before developing them. It is also the language of adventure because, when we say *"yes"* more, we suddenly find ourselves flung forward into places and situations we never expected. I had this experience in April 2013 when I found myself on stage at the London Comedy Store with seasoned improviser and TV/film star Neil Mullarkey, giving a talk on creativity and collaboration to a packed corporate audience. Whilst I've given many talks, this was a rather unique venue, collaborator and situation that I'd never before found myself in which was both exciting and a little scary. One of my lasting memories is of how bright the lights were – it was like giving a talk to the spaceship from *Close Encounters of The Third Kind*! Immediately after the event, I went to have coffee with a friend who I hadn't seen for some time and, on explaining what I had just been doing, he asked me *"How on earth did you end up doing that?"* The question stopped me in my tracks. There was no easy answer. It had never been a specific goal of mine or part of an overall business plan or personal development strategy. As I reflected, I realised that I had ended up having this rather unique experience simply through saying *"yes"* more where it would have been a hell of a lot easier and safer to say *"no."* There were a series of offers I had said *"yes"* to that led up to the Comedy Store gig. Offers that made me both excited and scared at the same time as I felt that accepting them would take me out of my comfort zone. Something inside me though, maybe my growing creative spirit, decided to say *"yes"* anyway and embrace and make sense of whatever mess would follow.

I paused and reflected on the choices that I had made to end up in this situation. I ended up at the Comedy Store because I said *"yes"* to Neil's invitation to collaborate with him. I'd met Neil a couple of years previously because I had said *"yes"* to the invitation of a fellow student at Ashridge Business School who invited me to an experimental Business Improvisation Lab that Neil was co-leading. I'd met my fellow student, Asher, at Ashridge because a year earlier I'd said *"yes"* to Professor Bill Critchley who had suggested that I should sign up for the Masters in Organisational Change programme that he ran.

I'd met Bill 18 months earlier because I'd said *"yes"* to a spare ticket an old boss had to a seminar Bill was giving on complex change. I was working for this boss because a couple of years earlier I'd said *"yes"* to an invitation to take on a challenging sideways move into a new role with a lot more responsibility but no extra reward. Within a few minutes of reflection I was able to trace the exciting event

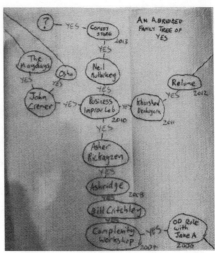

at The Comedy Store back through a family tree of *yes* to around 2007 – six years of *yes*! I drew out the family tree on a

napkin and then realised that this wasn't simply a linear path of a *yes* giving birth to a single new opportunity but a plethora of tangential multiple opportunities spawned exponentially from each *yes* like a family tree. At various points along the tree I met other people or came across other things to say *"yes"* to, forming new branches of *yes* – I soon ran out of space on the napkin! As I looked at the family tree of *yes* I was horrified at how fragile this chain of wonderful events had been. What if I'd said *"no"* at any point along the way? I remember having some anxiety about each of the decisions I made as they took me out of my comfort zone and I remember how easy it would have been to keep myself safe by simply saying *"no."*

I told Rob Poynton of my *yes* family tree and he responded by saying *"No kills children!"* My immediate interpretation of this phrase was that saying *"no"* to the creative ideas of children kills their childlike creative spirit. Whilst this is true, Rob's point was rather more profound – *"Saying no to an idea not only kills that idea but it kills its children – the other ideas that it would have given birth to had we said 'yes' to it."* This rang very true. Had I said *"no"* to taking on that role in 2007, not only would I have not had a challenging and rewarding couple of years of work but I would not have met Bill Critchley, nor gone to Ashridge, nor met Asher, nor met Neil, nor ended up at The Comedy Store or met a plethora of great people along the way that led to innumerable Creative Adventures, starting my own business and eventually writing this book.

I have since adopted Rob's *"No kills children"* idea as a personal mantra and a core principle for my innovation work. Often it seems that we are premature in our desire to see if a creative idea will work, scale or have a decent return on investment and we say *"no"* far too early. Novel ideas, especially the wacky, surreal and out-there ones are very fragile. They need nurturing, love, food and warmth and, whilst they may appear ugly or unusual when they are first born, it is only when they start to grow and mature that we can begin to see potential in them. It is for this reason that I think the *"Ugly* *Duckling"*[4] should be core reading for anyone interested in learning about innovation! (That and *"Oh, The Thinks You Can Think"*[5] by Dr Seuss!) In the early stages of innovation, it is often the case that the initial idea doesn't necessarily end up as a product or service, but the chain of thought it prompts or the challenges it presents are the catalyst needed to stimulate the imagination to come up with something special. I believe that any idea has the potential to grow if it is given enough love, light and *yes*.

A practice that I find helps prevent ideas being killed too early is to treat them as question marks, not exclamation marks. All too often it seems we have an instinctive desire to rapidly turn a concept or idea into an action, a decision or a conclusion as soon as possible – turn it into reality, turn it into a fact, resolve and conclude it. I suspect that this is due to the psychological anxiety that leaving things open and unresolved causes us, an anxiety that drives us to try and turn imaginative concepts and ideas into exclamation marks! Exclamation marks have no creative juices left in them to grow. Exclamation marks are dead. An exclamation mark is simply a question mark with rigamortis! A question mark, however, is alive and is vibrating with possibility, depth and adventure. The more we can treat ideas as question marks, presents to be unpacked that have further question marks within them, the more our ideas can flourish and turn into something special. And not only does this keep our ideas alive and growing but it paves the way for many generations of ideas that will be spawned from us saying *yes* more.

Experiment: "*Yes*" family trees

- *Bring to mind something in your life that you are particular proud of or something that you are really excited and energised about. Write it down in a bubble.*
- *Ask yourself what you had to say "yes" to in order for that to happen and add that to the previous generation of the yes family tree.*
- *Ask yourself the same question about that event - what did you have to say "yes" to in order for that to happen. Continue to expand the yes family tree as far back as possible. It might be that there is more than one parent for each child - expand these as far as possible.*
- *When you have exhausted your piece of paper take a step back and reflect on what you have drawn: What wouldn't have happened if you had said "no" at any point? At what points would it have been easier to say "no" or where others where encouraging you to say "no"? What makes a "yes" more difficult for you? What choices do you have right here and right now that it would be easy to say "no" to? What might happen if you said "yes" to them?*

It is impossible to get this experiment wrong – just be curious as to what you notice.

Saying "Yes" to Safe Uncertainty

I've been commuting into London on a fairly regular basis for a number of years now. Despite occasional delays and frustrations I do actually enjoy it. I get to read different books, get to see different people, get to visit different places and the nature of a big city such as London means that something unexpected or unusual is normally going on. As somebody interested in people, novelty and creativity it is a wonderful experience. However, something about my commuting experience bothers me and I feel the need to confess! If I am so welcoming of adventure why do I stand at the *same* place on the train platform, get on the *same* carriage and seek out the *same* seat every time I travel? (My secret commuter tactic here is to stand on a particular paving slab that I have learnt aligns exactly with the first set of train doors that are nearest to the seats that are normally empty. I like to think of this as the *slab of certainty*!) I know I'm not alone here as I see the majority of other commuters exhibit similar behaviour. It is somewhat Pavlovian in nature as our logical brain seems to tell us *"If I stand here, then the doors will be right in front of me"* or *"I can get on first an get a seat!"* or *"This carriage is far less crowded than the others"* or *"If I get on here then I will be in the right position for the exit when I get off"* (Imagine all of that said with the tonality and facial expression of a salivating Labrador expecting a treat!)

These benefits may be valid most of the time but I have also seen and experienced the somewhat ridiculous panic if something changes even just a little. Commuters can be sent into high anxiety states if a train brakes slightly too early or too late and the doors are not in their usual alignment with the platform. I've seen commuters stare with hatred and jealousy in their eyes if somebody *new* is standing in their place on the platform or even worse…sitting in their usual seat. I recall a time when the front set of doors on a packed Waterloo and City tube train failed to open and people looked ashen, saying to each other *"What are we going to do?"* as if they were trapped in a leaking submarine 20,000 leagues under the sea, despite the fact that every other set of doors was functioning correctly! (For those who aren't familiar with the London Underground, the Waterloo and City line only has two stops so it is highly unlikely the train is going to dash off anywhere until everybody has had time to disembark.)

It seems to me that the vast majority of us commuters want our commute to be unsurprising, predictable and without incident. Arguably there is nothing wrong with this and I recognise it in myself as coming from a desire to be in a place of *safe certainty* – a state in which I feel that I know what is going to happen and I know what to do when it does. In order to maintain this position of safe certainty I need to say *"no"* to possibility, novelty and difference and I am usually rewarded with a seat, an un-crowded carriage or simply not having to think and improvise so early in the morning. During my commute, I seem to have convinced myself that the alternative of this predictable, controllable norm is a place of *unsafe uncertainty* – a state in which I would have no idea of what is going to happen and wouldn't know how to respond when it did! Whilst a place of *unsafe uncertainty* might be a tiny bit appealing due to the novelty it would bring, my norm of *safe certainty* is the lesser of two evils and I have decided that it is better to sacrifice the possibility of adventure in favour of making it more likely that I will get a seat.

This is a ridiculous scenario as I think about it – the risks here are so incredibly low and the absolute worst that could happen is that I would have to walk a little, queue for a matter of seconds to get on board or stand and be a bit squashed for 26 minutes. I realise that what I have done with regard to my commute is *exactly* what I strive to warn others of in my coaching and consulting work – the habit of giving up possibility and opportunity in favour of certainty and predictability in a way that keeps everything rather stuck. If I were to practice what I preach with my commuting habits I would tell myself that there is a sweet spot between these two extremes – a place that psychologist Barry Mason calls *safe uncertainty*[6]. A state in which I wouldn't always know what was going to happen but in which I could still assure myself that I'm protected from major risk. *Safe uncertainty* is the fertile ground where creativity, innovation, adventure and change can grow and flourish.

Adapted from the works of Mason, Stacey, Critchley, Vanstone

Safe uncertainty is about being comfortable with the world of *just enough-ness*. It is about having *just enough* structure, *just enough* control and *just enough* planning to mitigate only the biggest of risks whilst leaving enough fluidity, spontaneity and freedom to welcome new possibilities. In organisational terms, a culture of *safe uncertainty* is one where folk are encouraged, within negotiated parameters, to try something new and if it doesn't work to then fail happy and learn from the experience. A team who are comfortable with *safe uncertainty* are great at predicting and planning but also masterful at adapting and improvising. Individuals who live their lives from a place of *safe uncertainty* are able to have wild adventures, learn new skills and develop new talents whilst being able to find novel ways of continuing to pay the mortgage, bring up kids, lead an active social life and not die through misadventure (etc). In other words, finding our own unique place of *safe certainty* helps us to say *"yes"* more.

Where you position yourself on this makeshift matrix is up to you, no position is right and no position is wrong (it is only a model after all!) However, if you are seeking novelty, adventure and change, but find yourself maintaining the status quo in the bottom left hand corner, then you may need to ask yourself *"What am I prepared to let go of?"* and *"What are the small, modest experiments I can undertake to gently move into the fertile safe uncertainty zone?"*

Summary: Say "Yes" (to the mess)

Whilst *no* is the language of safety and certainty, *yes* is the language of possibility, creativity and adventure. This practice is about becoming more aware of where our biases lie and, no matter how they are balanced, to tip them further towards *yes*. It is about realising that by saying *"yes"* we are acknowledging and accepting possibility and the fact that we will go far fast through doing this. It is about willingly seeking out *the mess*

92

and getting good at spotting the creative clues that are lurking in the metaphorical fog. It is about finding our own unique zone of safe uncertainty, deciding how much of a creative adventure we would like to embark on and how quickly we would like to get there.

Say "Yes" (to the mess)	
Let go	• Habitually saying *"no."* • Over analysing whether *yes* is a good idea or not. • Craving *safe certainty.*
Be more	• Spontaneously *"yes."* • Friendly with the *mess.* • Comfortable with *safe uncertainty.*
Experiment by	• Gradually saying *"yes"* more, especially to scary things. • Creating historical and futuristic yes *family trees.* • Leaping and then looking.

Chapter 5 References

1 Danny Wallace (2006) *"Yes Man: A Book About Saying Yes."* London: Ebury Press

2 Keith Johnston (1981) *"Impro - Improvisation and the Theatre."* London: Methuen

3 Frank Barrett (2012) *"Say Yes To The Mess: Surprising Leadership Lessons From Jazz."* Boston: Harvard

4 Hans Christian Andersen (1854) "The Ugly Duckling"

5 Dr Seuss (1975) *"Oh, the Thinks you can Think."* Random House Children's Book

6 Barry Mason (1993) *"Towards Positions of Safe Uncertainty"* in *Human Systems: The Journal of Systemic Consultation & Management Vol 4.*

Chapter 6 Be Obvious, Be Altered

Letting go of a need to be clever, original and impervious to the influence of others

"No question is so difficult to answer as that to which the answer is obvious."   *George Bernard Shaw (1856-1950)*

In March 2008 I flew to Ireland to facilitate a quarterly meeting for a group of 30 leaders of a manufacturing organisation.  I'd been worrying about this session for quite some time. I knew that although they were a reasonably friendly bunch, the majority of the male-dominated group were prone to stereotypical alpha male tendencies when things got tense and meetings often ended up drifting away from their purpose and into competitions for individual dominance. They'd asked me to facilitate in order to help with this dynamic and I'd crafted a number of exercises and experiences to blend into their agenda to help them surface and work on these habitual patterns. Despite my nervousness, I felt pleased with myself as I'd some good exercises, models and content up my sleeve that I felt would help them and impress them at the same time. After all, I wanted to work with this group again beyond this initial session. It was a two day meeting and day one went very well. It seemed my proposed agenda was hitting the mark and the group appeared to be working in a much more collaborative way. However, about half way through day two, things went completely off track. A plenary session somehow got into a debate that then turned into an argument and took us completely off topic and caught me by surprise. I decided to let the argument run for a bit to see what happened but after about 10 minutes the conversation was so far from where we had started that I began to feel lost. Tempers frayed, fingers wagged and voices became raised and accusational. The leader of the group kept glancing at me as if to say *"come on Steve – sort this out"*. This caused me to go completely into my head and start thinking of things I could do or say. Maybe there was a tool I could use, maybe I could talk about a model that would help them, I could set up an exercise or suggest some way for them to break into groups to do some work. All of these clever ideas felt wrong. I began to panic. More and more people looked towards me. Finally, out of total desperation, I stepped forward and said to the group *"I'm going to be honest with you guys here. I've absolutely no idea what to do. I'm totally lost and you're all looking to me to sort it out. You are going to have to help me out. What is it you need right now?"* I remember feeling flushed as I said this and thinking to myself *"I've blown it!"* I stood there facing a silence that seemed to last for ever. Some of the group looked confused as if to say *"It's your job to sort us out!"* However, others paused and reflected on what I'd said. Then one or two spoke up to say *"I agree. I've no idea what we're doing."* A few more agreed and articulated what they needed to help them out of their stuckness. Then, all of a sudden, a new conversation emerged in which the group began to collaborate in order to seek clarity and to work out what to do next. The rest of the day involved some tough, but genuine conversations that became a defining moment for the group in terms of their own development - a moment that didn't come from any masterful, well thought through or pre-planned intervention I had learnt from a guru or from a model in a book, but a moment that came about because, at point in time, the only personal resource I had left to rely on was to name what was *obvious* to me. Somehow, my obviousness positively *altered* the way the participants interacted with each other from that point on.

Being obvious

The most unhelpful thing to do in order to become more creative is to try harder! Trying harder to be more original or clever simply results in us becoming even more creatively stuck due to the mental effort we're having to exert. Creativity is elusive and the moment we try to find it and tame it, it seems to disappear. (It is like the floaty things that we occasionally see drifting across our vision – the moment we try to look at them they move away!) The key to tapping into our innate creativity is to simply become more obvious. Being obvious is the opposite of being original or clever. We often attempt to be original or clever when we are under pressure or want to impress others, particularly those we perceive to be in a position of power or those who we wish to influence. On reflection, I went into the Ireland experience with a desire to be original and clever to impress a bunch of leaders whom I perceived had power and influence over me. However, trying to be original or clever generally means we are relying on our logical brains to think us out of trouble. This results in us self-censoring and modifying our rather less eloquent, spontaneous thoughts and instincts and turning them into a script or a performance for others. However simple it may sound, being obvious is not easy. Ironically, it takes a lot of courage to be obvious as it is the antithesis of how many of us have been taught to respond under pressure.

Being obvious is about simply becoming more confident that our raw, basic, spontaneous ideas, reactions and insights are

of greater value to others than our well rehearsed pre-thought. Often our obviousness can feel pathetic, trivial or pointless but if we expose others to it they generally find it agreeable at worst but amazingly insightful, supportive or inspiring at best. As we are all uniquely individual human beings, what is obvious to us can be highly original or helpful to others. I have discovered that *Be Obvious* is a simple yet powerful mantra for developing one's creative spirit. Keith Johnstone suggests that *"The more you try to be creative the less obvious you are being. If you are completely obvious then you are the most unique person in the world and you amaze us."*[1] The more I've studied the art of the obvious, the more I've come to believe that genius is simply a state of being confident with one's obviousness. I doubt Einstein came up with any of his famous quotes and thought to himself *"I'd better jazz this one up a bit in order to make myself sound more clever and intelligent!"* He was simply confident in expressing his own obviousness and had a growing audience to expose it to.

"What is the most obvious thing to do?" has become one of my favourite coaching questions as well as one I ask myself on a daily basis. It doesn't guarantee success though, as being obvious demands a genuine response of ourselves that is uniquely of that moment in time and will therefore provoke unknown consequences. Getting comfortable with our own obviousness is a marvellous way of unsticking our stuckness and stepping into a more creative and adventurous space. It allows us to begin to trust our own spontaneous responses as a reliable source of what to do next. In my experience, what is obvious at any moment is usually what is needed. The

advantage of learning the art the obvious is that it requires far less effort, energy and brainpower than trying to be clever.

Experiment: The art of the obvious

- *Bring to mind as many problems, opportunities or personal goals as you can. Write them down.*
- *For each of them ask yourself "What is the most obvious thing to do?" Try to suspend, logic, reasoning and judgement and simply write down the first spontaneous thought that comes to mind. Note that your obvious thing does not need to totally resolve anything but simply help clarify or take a tiny step in the right direction. Having done this, it is likely the next obvious step will then appear.*
- *Once you have done this for each item, reflect on the whole list of obvious things. When and how can you do them? What prevents you doing the most obvious thing right now? How does your obvious response make you feel? How is your obvious thinking different to your clever and original thinking? How is this helpful?*

It is impossible to get this experiment wrong – just be curious as to what you notice.

Being altered

The other half of this practice is about being altered. Being altered is about being genuinely changed by our experience of interacting with others. It is different to simply listening to another person and agreeing with them. It is about being totally present with others and allowing their obviousness to disturb and alter something within us, be that positive or negative, insightful or uncomfortable. It is about allowing our identity armour and our sense of self (see Chapter 2) to become semi-permeable so that our experience of others seeps into and influences our thoughts, actions and beliefs in the moment. Being altered is a fundamental part of human interaction that perpetually takes place at varying levels of consciousness. It is a dance of interaction as we respond in our own unique way to the gestures of others, be they words, actions or physical movements.

When somebody is un-altered by our interaction with them we may feel ignored or rejected. Conversely when somebody is altered, we feel that we have been acknowledged or that a significant interaction has occurred. There is something psychologically satisfying about the process of human beings altering each other – only our ethics, values and moral compass decides whether we consider it appropriate or not. If you bring to mind your favourite film, book or comic strip it is likely that it appeals to you because the characters are altered by each other throughout the story. The archetypal fairy-tale is about traditional power dynamics being altered - the evil witch suppresses the princess, the peasant boy dressed in rags overpowers the witch, the princess marries the peasant, the donkey becomes the special advisor to the king (etc.) Everyone is continually altered through their interactions with each other. The most dull films or comic strips I have come across are those where the characters remain un-altered.

 Jaws[2] is a film I could watch again and again simply because of the interaction between the three main characters on board the Orca who continually battle for status and alter each other. The Perfect Storm[3], on the other hand, appears to try and simulate this gripping dynamic on board the Andrea Gail but fails to do so because, although a lot happens, nobody is altered by their interactions. Similarly the comic strip Garfield,

although curiously popular, has failed to amuse me for many years on the basis that nothing seems to change from the first panel to the last.

The process of altering and being altered by somebody is a deeply relational experience that can foster trust and compassion between individuals. I have experienced this through the strong relationships I have very quickly built when performing comedy improvisation with people I hardly know. There is something about a willingness to be altered by each other in front of an audience that is deeply bonding. For example, if I walk onto stage with an idea that I am going to be King Henry VIII and my fellow actor speaks first and says *"Mr Jenkins, I've got your test results, I'm afraid it is bad news"* then in a split second, for the scene to work and my partner to feel supported, I have to allow myself to let go of my pre-thought and become Mr Jenkins. I could find a clever way of blending my pre-thought into this new reality, by saying *"You mean the tests to confirm whether I am in fact the reincarnation of Henry VIII?"* but that feels like a lot of effort and means that both myself and my fellow performer are going to have to work really hard to keep the scene alive. The obvious thing to say would be something like *"Oh my goodness doctor, please tell me you are joking!"* but to do this I need to allow myself to be altered by the other person. I find that if I'm not enjoying an improvisation show it is usually because the players are not allowing themselves to be altered by each other and, rather than observing a wonderful display of raw human interaction, I am simply experiencing a series of unconnected individual statements that are plopped on top of one other.

I notice a similar lack of excitement and liveliness when observing or participating in many corporate rituals such as meetings, workshops or off-site events. It seems to me that often these occasions have been rather a waste of time, money and energy as nobody is altered by them. People may leave feeling like they have worked hard but they are essentially exactly the same as they went in – they've simply kept themselves busy. However, the occasions where I have witnessed people being transformed and having profound breakthroughs have been those where the meeting or workshop has been structured in such a way that it has allowed enough space for people to be altered – to be changed by their experience of closely interacting with each other. On these occasions there is no need to type up minutes, or force out any key take-aways as the change has already taken place and the participants go forth and interact with others in their altered state.

The difference between *real* change and simply undertaking busy work can be thought of as the difference between action and interaction. Action is where we engage in a lot of activities that feel like we are exerting effort and keeping ourselves busy (e.g. following an agenda, giving a presentation, brainstorming or following reductionist meeting ground rules that keep everything *on track*.) These activities are satisfying because they match the description of what we have socially agreed good work looks and feels like. Action feels like we are in control, we are busy, we are exerting mental effort and moving at pace, but very little actually changes as a result. Action is informed by a chronos perspective of time (see Chapter 3). Action focuses on an amount of busy-ness to be fitted into a set period of time which generally means we have few opportunities to be altered by the experience, let alone pause, breath or allow moments of helpful, creative silence to creep in.

Interaction, however, is where we engage with each other, make our relationships the collective focus of our attention and allow ourselves to be altered whilst we simultaneously alter others. We may do this through traditional forms of work such as making decisions, solving problems or having conversations but with a very different pace and rhythm that is less structured, less controlling and more emergent. Interaction is informed by a kairos perception of time (see Chapter 3) where the flow of meaning and emergent needs decide when the work is finished as opposed to a pre-defined agenda.

When designing meetings, workshops or conferences, instead of asking clients what business outcomes they would like, I have taken to asking them *"How do you want people to be altered by this experience?"* I have began using a three panel comic strip-esque template to help facilitate this conversation, illustrating what state we imagine people will begin in, what state we'd ideally like them to finish in and then how we intend to make it *most likely* for people to be altered in the middle. (I have to emphasise my use of the words *most likely* here as there can never be any guaranteed result due to the complex nature of our relationships with others). Often clients end up concluding that their planned agenda will not achieve their desired outcome and we might redesign it from a more kairos informed perspective. Occasionally they conclude that they don't actually want anyone to be altered in which case I politely suggest that they don't really need my help! Keith Johnston uses the term *gossip* to describe the difference between action and interaction. *"There is no interaction when nobody is altered. This is just gossip. Gossip oils people so they can slide past each other without grinding up against them."*[1]

As human beings, we tend to resist being altered as to be altered creates a perceived letting go of our sense of selves. However, through allowing ourselves to be *appropriately* altered, we begin to create the psychological movement needed to disturb our sense of selves enough to allow our creative spirit to emerge through the gaps created.

Experiment: Being altered

- *Try to become hyper-aware of where you and others are altered by each other by paying close attention to the offers and responses to offers that occur, be they words, sounds, physical postures or movements.*
- *Observe how people are interacting. How do the offers of one person alter the response of the other? Does it have an impact or does it seem to have no effect at all?*
- *Observe yourself and notice as people interact with you whether you are altered or if you resist being altered.*
- *Bring to mind a person or type of person who you are most willing to be altered by and a person or type of person who you typically resist. What is it about each of them that causes you to respond in this way?*
- *Reflect on the following questions: What lies behind this resistance or acceptance? What would happen if you allowed yourself to be altered in situations that you normally resist and vice versa? What patterns do you notice in who and how you block or accept?*

It is impossible to get this experiment wrong – just be curious as to what you notice.

The creative dance of Be Obvious and Be Altered

This practice is yin and yang in its nature. It has two elements that are each present in the other for a simple reason - the whole is greater than the sum of the parts. Combining the two practices and simultaneously nurturing the art of the obvious whilst allowing ones self to become altered by the obviousness of others is not only a great way to develop our creative abilities but also a powerful way of developing relationships and groups.  Teams that are able to be obvious with each other whilst being altered by each other's obviousness tend to have a much more lively, flexible and creative dynamic. They may argue more, debate more and fall out with each other regularly as, at least in the early days of their development, obviousness might result in a difficult level of honesty being voiced for the first time. However, with practice, they are able to quickly recover, innovate, create and change together much more easily.

On many occasions, I've simply worked on developing the *Be Obvious, Be Altered* practice with groups - encouraging participants to get more confident at being obvious whilst allowing themselves to be altered when others do the same. This is a particularly important practice to develop when looking to stimulate an organisational culture of creativity and innovation as it reduces the unhelpful pressure to be clever and original which stifles the very process one is trying to stimulate. It also creates a highly supportive culture of collaboration. I'm always amused that, at school, this process of sharing our work and using other people's stuff is outlawed as *cheating* but, in the workplace, the very same process is called *collaboration*! This may yield some clues as to why the dance of *Be Obvious Be Altered* is so tricky for educated adults to master.

Experiment: The dance of the obvious and altered

- *Find somebody to have a conversation with and agree that the only two objectives of this conversation are to be obvious (i.e. trusting and then acting on your spontaneous response) and to be altered (i.e. allowing yourself to be spontaneously changed by the obvious responses of the other.*
- *You can talk about anything you like, however it is a more powerful experiment if you can talk about something that is real, important, consequential or exciting to you both.*
- *Continue to talk until the conversation comes to a natural end or you start to find things too difficult to continue.*
- *Reflect on your experience of the conversation: How did it feel? Where was it more easy or more difficult? What helped and what hindered? What did you notice about yourself that may be a clue to help you become more obvious and more willing to be altered? How did being obvious feel for you? How did you experience the obviousness of the other?*

It is impossible to get this experiment wrong – just be curious as to what you notice.

Summary: Be Obvious, Be Altered

 This practice is about becoming more aware of where we habitually censor or modify what is obvious to us in order to be perceived as clever or original. It is about noticing where these habits cause us to operate to a script that stifles our spontaneous selves and slowly dampens our creative spirit. It is about placing a greater value on naming the obvious as a way of establishing what is uniquely demanded by any particular moment. It is also about simultaneously noticing where we allow ourselves to be altered by others and where we resist being altered. It is about realising that, if we allow ourselves to be altered by others, then we are rarely left not knowing what to say or do. Through nurturing our ability to be simultaneously obvious and altered we create a mutually supportive environment in which our creative spirits can begin to flourish and shine in front of each other.

Be Obvious, Be Altered	
Let go	• The need to be clever or original. • Our resistance to being changed by others. • Logical and rational thought as our default *modus operandi*.
Be more	• Trusting that one's obvious response is what the present moment demands. • Semi-permeable. • Welcoming of the disturbance others brings to our own perceptions.
Experiment by	• Being as obvious as possible. • Allowing yourself to be altered as much as possible by others. • Use other people's stuff!

Chapter 6 References

[1] From conversations with Keith Johnstone in London 2012

[2] Jaws (1975) Directed by Stephen Spielberg

[3] The Perfect Storm (2000) Directed by Wolfgang Petersen

Chapter 7   Fail Happy
Letting go of our need to perpetually succeed

"If you're not making a mistake, it's a mistake!"
                    Miles Davis (1926-1991)

I love to doodle when I take notes. In fact, my page is often less words and more doodles. I find it gives my notes colour and life and I remember more about the occasion than if they were simply a list of sterile, dead bullet points. One thing that I've never been able to draw very well though are human faces. I can do cartoon ones reasonably well but not *proper* ones. When I see people who are able to do this I am extremely impressed and a little envious. I often watch how they do it and then try to imitate their actions but it never comes out the same. I really wanted to learn how to do this so I recently asked a talented friend what their secret was, expecting him to respond by giving me tips about face ratios, techniques for sculpting expressions or a guide to realistic facial contour shading. He responded by telling me *"It's easy. You have to screw it up at least 1,000 times in order to learn how not to do it – after that it becomes much easier!"*

As a society we have a funny relationship with failure. For me, no matter how much I want to become good at drawing faces, I want to be able to do it quickly. If I try to begin drawing 999 less than perfect ones I tend to get disheartened after five poor efforts and inevitably find a reason to give up and do something else, suddenly remembering there was an important job to do around the house or that the cat needed his medicine a little early today. On the odd occasion that I manage to draw one reasonably well and get confident, the next one inevitably is not as good and I give up. I instinctively know that to get good at drawing faces failure is necessary, however I still can't bring myself to embrace it as a source of learning. I am suspicious that deep down, drawing faces simply isn't important enough for me to tolerate the amount of failure needed to get good at it.

This practice is about developing a greater willingness to try something new, knowing that you have a good chance of failing and, if you do, to fail happy in the knowledge that you have learnt something. It is about celebrating when things come out not quite as you planned. It is about rejoicing in those moments when your mind goes completely blank and you've no idea what to do, especially if it is in front of others. If I pause and mine the present moment (see Chapter 3) for clues as to why I sometimes find it difficult to fail happy I once again find experiences from school lurking in the depths of my subconscious. Memories of mathematics loom large as I remember opening my homework exercise book with a cringe on my face and a racing heart because I knew a plethora of red crosses awaited me. No matter how many times this happened, I always held a tiny glimmer of hope that it would be full of praise but it never was. Rather than my teachers celebrating each cross as a discovery, an uncovering of something that I didn't yet know, something that was new to me that I could learn and work out in partnership with them, my efforts were simply marked as wrong and I was sent back to re-read the same text book that had confused me in the first place. I had similar experiences getting art, drama and music *wrong* and I'm sure there are many other occasions over the years where a fear of failure has bullied my creative spirit into quiet submission. Through early education and then into my working career I learnt that failure is not a sign of potential but a sign of weakness that must be overcome or hidden at all costs.

This practice helps us to gently quieten our *mustn't fail* mantra by teaching us to place a greater trust in our instinctive, spontaneous selves and to refrain from berating the creative genius within us if something doesn't turn out as we'd hoped it would. However, it isn't about deliberately setting out to fail. It is about letting go of our fears, trying something new and trusting that, at some point, our instinctive, spontaneous selves will screw up when a significant learning opportunity emerges. I like to think of this process of seeking and then embracing failure as developing our own personal discovery radar.

Of course, a balance needs to be struck here as there are things that we do not want to fail at because it may result in catastrophe (death, injury etc.) so failing happy is about conducting some personal, small, modest experiments. Experiments that, should they end up going spectacularly wrong, we could live with the consequences (See *Must Look First lists* in Chapter 2.) I have found that developing a deeper, genuine curiosity lies at the heart of becoming more willing and able to fail happy. Becoming more curious about ourselves, our interests, our passions, our hobbies and our lives in general provides an incredible source of resilience, energy and motivation. If we are passionately curious about something then the pain of failure seems to be more bearable. I like to think of the following crude formula to describe the importance of curiosity in nurturing an ability to fail happy.

10% more curiosity = 10% more bravery = 10% more experimentation = 10% more Creative Adventures and 10% more happy failures

Finding the Failure Threshold

I'd been toying with the idea of using theatrical masks in my innovation workshops for a while as they are a great mechanism for allowing us to play with perceptions of our own identity and limiting beliefs. They are also a bit creepy and not the typical thing you encounter in the corporate world, which I also found rather appealing. There is something about a mask and the partial anonymity it brings that allows the wearer to activate and tap into parts of themselves that have long lay dormant, bypassing the internal mad, bad and wrong PR department. It was with this in mind that I decided it would be a good idea to experiment with masks at the next workshop I was running.

However, as the day approached I started to notice I was getting rather anxious *"What if it doesn't work?"* I thought to myself. I began to wonder if it was a good idea and considered abandoning my experiment in favour of something safer but it was my deep, embodied curiosity that enabled me to be a little bit braver and try it out. The experiment was a fantastic success. The participants and I learnt a lot about ourselves and each other and I continue to use the mask exercise to this day. I felt delighted but then I realised I hadn't actually failed. This in itself wasn't a problem, but what I realised was that I would have to deepen my curiosity much further and be even braver with my experiments in order to screw up and find the real edge of my abilities. In other words, I realised that my fear of failure was causing me to be rather conservative – my actual failure threshold was much further out-there than I had perceived.

With this in mind, I ran another workshop a few weeks later that not only involved masks but also paints, crayons, musical instruments and I played the role of a cloaked character called the *Creative Disturber* who challenged participants in a way that ended up unintentionally coming across as eerie and quite disconcerting!  Before this workshop I was again worried that it would go wrong and I would be deemed a failure but my curiosity gave me the momentum and resilience to give it a go. The day came, I bravely began the workshop and it ended up being pretty much a total disaster! The participants were supposed to leave feeling like inspired creatives, instead they left feeling rather confused and disturbed. Two participants went as far as describing the workshop as *"like being in a living nightmare"* and *"like experiencing the final moments of a disintegrating society!"* (Note: although the participants found the experience of *that workshop* very weird, as far I am aware nobody was permanently mentally or physically damaged). However, even though this experiment didn't turn out as I'd hoped it would I had found the edge, I discovered how far I needed to deepen my curiosity to make it not work and, in doing so, I had a plethora of insights that I would never have had if I had played it safe. Some modified bits of the workshop have subsequently worked very well.

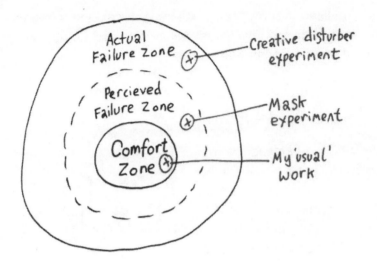

Actual Failure Zone (+) ——— Creative disturber experiment

Percieved Failure Zone (+) ——— Mask experiment

Comfort Zone (+) ——— My 'usual' work

It was a failure and, at the time, I hated the experience of failing so publicly. However, with the benefit of hindsight and reflection, I came to realise it was a happy failure because the whole experiment was driven by my deep curiosity and raised some new questions, insights and ideas that I would never have had got had I listened to my overly conservative inner critic. I have since found that the more I experience failure, whilst I still don't particularly enjoy it, I am quicker to realise the learnings and move to a feeling of curious discovery. A more accurate way of describing this practice would be *Fail.......Happy* as it is about reducing the time delay between the two words as opposed to striving to experience happiness and failure simultaneously.

Experiment: The fruitful Fail Happy zone

- *On a piece of paper draw the three concentric circles shown on the previous page.*
- *In the middle circle list three to five things that you know you can do and you feel are within your comfort zone.*
- *In the second circle list three to five things that you would like to do but don't believe you are able to. (Things that are not excluded by your Must Look First list from Chapter 2) For each of these, design a small, modest experiment that will test if you are right.*
- *Try out your experiments. If they work then congratulate yourself and, at the same time, realise that your perceived failure threshold is further out than you thought. Your next step is to design an experiment that is further out from this one.*
- *If your experiment fails then congratulate yourself on finding the rich edge of your own learning. Your next step is to reflect deeply to see what you have uncovered and how this might be useful in future experiments.*

It is impossible to get this experiment wrong – just be curious as to what you notice.

There are many stories of successful failures. Some of the more well known ones are the invention of a failed glue that didn't stick too well but eventually became Post-It notes, the pill designed to treat angina by relaxing blood vessels that failed clinical trails but had some unusual side effects and eventually became Viagra and the legend of Thomas Edison's 1,000 failed attempts to invent a light bulb. As Edison famously responded when questioned as to how it felt to fail so often *"I didn't fail 1,000 times, the light bulb was an invention of 1,000 steps!"*

The stigma of failure

Tim Smitt is the founder of the Eden Project in Cornwall that is described by many as the eighth wonder of the world. The project involved the construction of a number  of incredible, self-contained biospheres that house species of plants from all around the world in the often cold and rainy south-west of England. Smitt is often referred to as a visionary or an entrepreneur but emphasizes that Eden came about simply through an ability to dream, suggesting that his real talent was not coming up with the idea but a dogged determination to convince others to invest. He explains *"Is there not anyone aged 12 who didn't dream about Eden. That's not visionary. What is visionary is attempting to convince a world predisposed to say no!"*[1] He suggests that what stifles dreams such as Eden from becoming a reality is a fear of failure *"Britain is crap at being entrepreneurial because a) it's a risk averse country and b) the stigma of failure is so high that if you fail you're considered to be a loser."*[1]

On a daily basis we stifle our creative spirit because we are unable or unwilling to experiment and fail happy, be that taking the first steps towards our own vision of our life's work, right down to simple, everyday tasks like experimenting with how we cook dinner. Creative *Breakaway* Chef Eric Gower spoke to me about fear of failure in the kitchen *"Almost all cooks have six dishes that they cook and just keep doing over and over."* He believes that the key to breaking new ground and innovating is to come up with interesting new combinations and ask oneself *"I wonder if that would work? What's the*

worst that could happen? If it doesn't work then big *******
deal! You order a take away! The very act of not worrying
about it makes you a better cook."

Stoicism is a school of philosophy founded in Athens in 308BC that I first came across in Oliver Burkeman's book *"The Antidote – A Bracing detox for the self help junkie."[2]* As I understand it, the Stoic philosophy stresses the fundamental importance of *reason* in making sense of our moment by moment experience, replacing our irrational judgments with rational ones. What intrigues me about this philosophy is whether it can help us make more rational judgments about our own fear of failure and, in doing so, liberate our creative spirit. Turning our irrational fears into rational ones is not something that can be achieved theoretically or hypothetically but, as the Stoic philosopher Seneca suggests, by *"deliberately experiencing those evils so as to grasp that they might not be as bad as you'd irrationally feared."[2]* In other words, in order to begin to make friends with our fear of failure we have to find out where it lives, knock on the door and invite ourselves in for a long and somewhat uncomfortable chat!

Burkeman spent time with the American Psychologist Albert Ellis, whose rather unique approach to his work was influenced by the Stoics. Ellis taught him that the value of deliberately experiencing our fears is that we can better make the distinction *"between outcomes that*  *are completely terrible, versus those that are merely bad."[2]* Burkeman decided to experiment by experiencing the fear, discomfort and discovery that Ellis was referring to. He boarded a busy London Underground train on the Central Line with a mission to shout aloud the names of the approaching stations a moment before the automated announcer did. He explains that, whilst he initially felt very self-conscious and worried about the consequences of his actions, by the time that he arrived at the third station he crossed "*some kind of psychic boundary. The adrenaline subsides, the panic dissipates and I find myself confronting the truth that…none of this is anywhere near as bad as I'd been anticipating.*"[2]

The term *experiential learning* is used a lot in the corporate world nowadays, but what Ellis and Burkeman are referring to is something very different to the usual developmental programmes that feature role-play scenarios, scripted group tasks or field trips to visit a different company or culture. This type of experiential learning is about seeking out, experiencing and getting to know our fears in order to alter the judgements we make about how bad the consequences might be. As suggested in Chapter 2, the majority of fears that keep our creative spirit deeply frozen are social anxieties as opposed to anything life threatening so we can afford to experiment and get to know them a little better in order to ascertain if they are absolutely terrible or simply a little awkward.

Experiment: Absolutely terrible *versus* a little awkward

- *Bring to mind something that you are deeply curious about but are too scared to try because of the social anxieties you might experience if you were to fail (i.e. people might ridicule you or think you are mad, bad or wrong.) As illustrated by Oliver Burkeman's experiment, this can be as small and as simple as you like. The key thing is that you experience the fear.*
- *Write down what you think will happen: What will you feel like and how do you anticipate others will react?*
- *Try out your experiment and, whilst you do, be curious about the following: What are you thinking/feeling? What are others doing in response to your experimentation? How is this experience different to what you anticipated? How are the responses of others different to what you anticipated?*
- *Reflect on your experiment: Was the experience easier or more difficult than you anticipated? What were the biggest differences between the anticipated and the actual experience? How has this experiment been useful in helping you to work out the boundaries of your failure threshold? How did your curiosity about the experiment help? How has this experiment been helpful in discovering how to fail happy?*

It is impossible to get this experiment wrong – just be curious as to what you notice.

The unique gift of failure

My wife, daughter and I used to live in a flat in London that was lovely in every aspect apart from the fact that we had nightmare neighbours living above us whose perpetual noise permeated every part of our lives and made us all very  miserable. Out of desperation, we eventually sold our flat and moved to a rented house outside of London which we fell in love with. After six months, we had just began to feel settled when our landlord came to visit and dropped a bombshell – he had to sell the house and, as we couldn't afford the asking price, we had to leave. We felt heart-broken and set about finding a permanent home. Eventually we found somewhere and our hopes were once-again raised but, after many months of going through the elongated and bureaucratic purchasing process, it fell through. We were distraught. However a silver lining soon emerged and we found another property that, whilst not as ideal as our rental property, was better than the previous one. We once again began the painstakingly slow process of home ownership and, at the final hurdle, the whole thing collapsed again. It was a real low for us as a family – we had to imminently leave our dream home and couldn't find anything we loved as much despite trying so hard for almost a year. Something interesting then happened that wouldn't have happened if our previous two attempts to move had been successful. Our landlord, who had become a good friend over the time we had lived there, had a change of heart. Having seen our struggle and had time to evaluate the ever-volatile housing market, he offered to sell us our dream house for a price we could afford and we have happily lived there ever since.

Had we not experienced the failures we did, our outcome wouldn't have been so wonderful. Had our first or second move actually gone to plan, our landlord wouldn't have had the time to get to know us or change his mind. Had our plan gone to plan then we would have lost out! I realised through this experience that each time failure occurs, a new opportunity is simultaneously created – we simply may not realise what it is at the time. In a quest to help me become better at failing happy I have got into the habit of asking *"What is the unique gift that this failure has given birth to?"* and remind myself that it could take anything from a minute to a lifetime to work out what it is.

Summary: Fail Happy

This practice is about discovering where our fear of failure keeps our creative spirit in a deep freeze. It is about discovering how a deep and genuine curiosity about our own creative abilities can help us to become braver in trying stuff out that we think may not work. It is about realising that most of our fears are in fact social anxieties, worries about what others may think of us, that are essentially low risk and we can afford to experiment with more. It is about nurturing a belief that the only way we can make more accurate judgements about our creative selves is through experimentation and deeply experiencing whether our fear of failure is as bad as we thought. A lot of the time we may surprise ourselves in finding that we didn't actually fail and, on the occasions we do, we learn how to fail happy because we have discovered something valuable. It is about regarding failure not as a catastrophe, but simply the passing of an imagined future that didn't come to fruition. It is about developing our ability to reduce the time between failure and happiness through continually asking ourselves *"what gift does this newly shaped future hold for us?"* and taking great delight in trying to find the answer.

Fail Happy	
Let go	• Our need to know something will work before we are prepared to try it. • A perception that failure is a sign of weakness and must be avoided at all costs. • Our perceived (and likely very conservative) failure threshold.
Be more	• Deeply curious as to "what would happen if?" • Willing to experience the very things that we are trying to avoid to see if they are really bad or simply a bit awkward. • 10% more curious = 10% braver = 10% more experimental.
Experiment by	• Experiencing failure and asking oneself: "Was it as bad as I imagined?" • Experiencing failure and asking oneself: "What did I discover?" • Expecting failure but celebrating unplanned, accidental successes!

Chapter 7 References

1 Tim Smitt talking at Learnfest, Windermere UK 2013

2 Oliver Burkeman (2013) "*Antidote - A bracing detox for the self help junkie*" Edinburgh: Canongate Books Ltd

Chapter 8 Embody it
Challenging the dictatorship of the logical brain

"Lose your mind and come to your senses."
Fritz Perls

I'm always wary of bringing sporting stories into personal development work. The corporate world seems to be crammed full to  bursting-point with metaphors of sporting excellence or key-note speeches from ex-sportsmen and women who are keen to help us understand how their story is a relevant metaphor for the world of leadership, change, strategy, etc: *"Serving a Leadership Ace"*, *"Rowing to Strategic Excellence"*, *"Push the People Envelope and Feel the Leadership Burn"* to give some tongue-in-cheek examples! Whilst there is arguably nothing wrong with doing this in small doses, the habit of drawing on sports analogies seems to forget that not all of the population actually like sport and are therefore not inspired!

I say all of this because I am about to use sport, not as a metaphor, but as a way of exploring something that I feel is very relevant to creativity - the phenomena of *choking*. *Choking* is a term that describes the moment when somebody with world class ability and years of experience, fails at a very simple task that they have done many, many times before. As an Englishman, with a gradually waning interest in football, the immediate scenario that comes to mind is the performance of the national team in high-stakes penalty shoot-outs. For a highly experienced (and highly paid) professional footballer it shouldn't be too difficult to kick a ball 11 metres into a goal that is 7.3 x 2.4 metres. Fair enough, adding a goalkeeper makes it trickier to score a goal, but it should still be a relatively easy task to hit the ball on target, even if it is saved. Yet, for the last 22 years the England football team has struggled to win a shoot-out and forlorn fans have seen many spectacular, high-profile misses as balls have flown high and wide of the goal. So what is it that causes such talented individuals to choke when performing an arguably simple task? One of the main theories is that the pressure of the occasion leads to *over-thinking* which, in turn, leads to *under-performance*. This is where the sporting story blends into the everyday lives of regular human beings, as over-thinking and relying on our logical thought processes to stimulate our creative spirit can end up in us creatively choking!

In *"The Athlete's Way"*[1] Christopher Bergland suggests that we have two types of memory: *implicit memory* and *explicit memory*. Things that we learn to do through practice that become automatic, such as riding a bike or walking, are part of our implicit memory – a form of long term memory Bergland describes as *"memory that doesn't require conscious thought and is expressed by means other than words."* Explicit *memory* on the other hand is a more logic-driven *"declarative memory that is formed consciously and can be described in words."* The theory is that when athletes and sportspeople choke they are, for some reason, over-relying on their explicit memory and logical thought to such an extent that they de-tune from their more implicit and instinctive abilities. In my experience the same thing happens when we try too hard to think creatively.

This practice is about paying more attention to our bodies, senses and instincts and discovering that it is here that our creative spirit lives. It is about beginning to hand over the controls to the body and allowing our logical brains to take a back seat, contributing only when logical thought is genuinely helpful. It is about jumping up and trying something out even if it hasn't been thought through beyond noticing a curious sensation to act. At some point in our lives, even if it were as far back as early childhood, all of these creative practices came naturally to us so, somewhere in our psyche, these abilities are embedded within our implicit memory, we just need to stop trying so hard to think ourselves creative. This practice is about expanding our peripheral awareness beyond logical thought and taking seriously the plethora of clues and insights that our bodies and senses provide us with on a perpetual basis. It is about avoiding creatively choking by getting into a more symbiotic relationship with our bodies, senses and instincts once again.

The word *body* appears to be a bit of a taboo in the corporate world and it seems to me that we anaesthetise ourselves from the neck down as we pass through the office doors or factory gates. (The origins of the word *anaethesis* are Greek and literally mean *without sensation*.) The majority of adult human beings appear to regard their bodies as something that simply carries their head to the office and to various meetings and social occasions. Everything else it does is regarded as an inconvenience that must only be paid attention to behind closed doors or in front of a qualified medical practitioner when things start going wrong. It is like the head is a teenage son or daughter and the body is the parental taxi service, only called and woken up when a lift is needed or if there is a problem it cannot resolve. Looking at the increasingly worrying health statistics, cases of stress and expanding waistlines around the world it seems we need to redress this balance, not simply for creative benefits, but to prolong human life.

It is a taught and learnt behaviour to lead with our brains, head, and logical thought. We are taught at school and through our careers to evaluate situations logically and use deductive reasoning to inform the choices we make. In my coaching work I have had many people tell me that they have been told that, in order to progress in their careers, they need to be less emotional and more rational. Whilst I can understand that unprovoked emotional outbursts on inappropriate occasions could be problematic, our senses, emotions and intuitions can play a major role in how we make sense of our experience, problem solve and relate to each other. Many of those given the feedback to be less emotional seem to have decided that all sensual impulses are inappropriate and therefore have tuned out of their bodies completely. We have become so reliant on our logical brain chatter that the weaker signals from our bodies and senses are largely drowned out. However, if we are able to quieten the mind a little we can begin to better notice the rich information our bodies and senses are giving us in every moment.

Experiment: Handing over the controls

You will need an assistant for this experiment.

- *Stand up with your arm outstretched but relaxed.*
- *Your assistant is to push down on your outstretched arm with both hands. Do not resist, just allow it to happen.*
- *Repeat the exercise but this time tense all of your muscles as tight as possible in order to resist it being pushed down. This should be considerably more difficult to achieve than the previous step.*
- *Finally, repeat the exercise but this time relax your arm, relax your mind and trust that your body knows what to do in order to be strong. Keep it relaxed and simply let it imagine it is reaching for something. You may want to focus it by saying "arm be strong". If you successfully manage to adjust the locus of control from brain to body then it should be much more difficult to push down than either of the previous steps.*

It is impossible to get this experiment wrong – just be curious as to what you notice.

Given an opportunity, our bodies seem to intuitively know exactly what is going on and precisely what to do. This is forever apparent in extreme circumstances, such as disasters, where those who manage to escape describe the experience as being a bit of a blur, as if they acted on some sort of instinctive autopilot. These important and intuitive signals are there all the time, however it seems that we only notice them when they become exaggerated by a particular context. This practice is about getting good at noticing the perpetual signals our bodies and our emotions give out, no matter how weak they are. The physical experiment above helps highlight that the logical brain can relax a little more, safe in the knowledge that the body knows what to do. In step one of the experiment our logical brain is still in charge and choosing to allow the body to relax. In step two, the logical brain is still in control, but this time is ordering every single muscle that it is aware of to tense in order to prevent our arm from being pushed down. The trouble here is that half the muscles in our arm pull up and half pull down (i.e. we don't need to use them all in order to resist the push of the other) so we unintentionally help the other person achieve their objective. In step three we let the body decide what is needed as it knows exactly what muscles to tense and what muscles to relax in order to achieve the desired objective. We allow it to do what it needs in order to physically reach-out as opposed to forcing it to tense everything. If you managed to achieve this you may have surprised your logical brain and had it say "*Wow!*" This is a realisation that you have an incredibly complex and powerful intuiting and sensing machine sitting below your head. Imagine what the brain and body could do together if a truly mutual partnership was struck? (I must highlight here that this separation of body and brain as two separate, sometimes quarrelling siblings is of course only a simple, convenient metaphor to help explore something that is far more complex.)

Building trust with our bodies

It is one thing to have fun experiencing a martial arts party trick such as the arm challenge, but another to begin forming a deep trust of our body and senses as an important navigation aid for life and business. The first step to doing this is to gradually become more aware of our bodily sensations and how they manifest and change depending on the context we find ourselves in. The next step is to begin to trust them more. These thoughts were in my mind when I facilitated a strategy development session with a client in late 2012. The intention of the day was to gather the leadership team together in order to work out the strategic priorities and desired ways of working for the following year. Whilst I had a good sense of the background, the desired outcome of the session and what we *might* do during the time we had together, I had no other pre-conceived plans and decided I would experiment by trusting my instincts in-the-moment to help me work out what was needed. Whilst I had become more used to working in this way over recent times, I still noticed that I was mentally rehearsing scenarios in my head on the days leading up to the session, imagining how I would lead the day, what I would say and the types of responses or problems that may emerge. During the time leading up to the workshop my logical brain was bombarding me with signals that I needed to prepare more, write stuff down and plan! When this normally happens I translate it as a signal to start to begin working out a detailed agenda, flow and timings but, just as I was about to sit down and start to do this, I decided to pay attention to my body and noticed that it felt loose and relaxed. I can only describe that it felt in a state of flow as if it was telling me that everything was in control and I needn't worry, as it knew exactly what it was doing. I decided therefore to not sit down and prepare despite my logical brain seeming to ask me *"Are you sure this is a good idea?"* This happened a couple of times during the build up to the session, but again I noticed how my body appeared loose and unconstrained so I chose not to take the time to prepare.

On the day itself, whilst sitting on the train on the way into the client's office, I noticed that my body felt tight in the shoulders and a little restricted, which I took as a sign that I needed to do some preparation to alleviate my instinctive anxiety. I decided that I'd spend some time working out what I'd write on the flip chart so that the attendees would get an orientation of the day when they arrived. When I got to the venue, I wrote the flow for the day on a flip chart, the team arrived and we had a very productive, valuable and improvised *live* day together. This was the smallest amount of preparation I had ever done for such a session and I subsequently realised how much time, effort and energy I normally put into mentally rehearsing in advance. I must emphasise a difference here between preparation that is needed to ensure that one is clear on the clients needs, context and outcomes versus preparation that is unnecessarily being demanded by our own logical brain to make us feel better. I realised, in this instance, that my need to plan was simply a need of my logical brain to feel like I had done enough planning. As Colonel Tom Colditz once said *"Plans are proof that planning has been done!"* By paying attention to my body and letting it take the lead I believe it helped me realise my confidence and told me that it was OK to rely on my own spontaneity in this situation. In his book *"Flow"*[2] Mihaly Csikszentmihalyi talks of a harmony that must be achieved between the body, the senses and the mind to truly work in a state of flow – a state of ease, grace, excitement and achievement. He describes the symbiotic nature of flow using examples of how athletes need great mental discipline to achieve physical feats, but also how great chess players undertake a physical training regime to improve their levels of concentration.

During the strategy session itself I decided to continue allowing my body to take more of a lead than I usually would. Within the first 10 minutes, as we sat around the table talking about how we felt and our desired outcomes of the day, I noticed that I was starting to feel constrained around my upper body. I felt like I wanted to stand up, move about more and make big sweeping movements with my arms, so I decided to suggest something more creative and physically stimulating. I suggested to the group that they stand around three big sheets of paper that I had placed on the tables and co-create rich pictures of what it was like to work in the organisation. Now, working with groups using rich pictures isn't new to me, but it was the metaphorical conversation that occurred between my body and my mind in helping me decide what to do that I found most interesting. After the session, I imagined the conversation between my logical brain and my body and drew a cartoon in my journal to represent the symbiosis I felt was going on.

After a few nervous glances at each other, which I imagined being a result of logical brains trying to make sense of what I had just suggested, the group sprang into life, breathing some wonderful creative insights into a subject that could equally have been very dull and stuck. I'll never know if the bodies of other participants were giving them similar signals, but ever since this session I have started to use my own sensuous experience and somatic responses to a situation to offer me clues as to what is needed at any particular moment.

Experiment: Tuning into our senses

- On a piece of paper draw two columns labelled as: "Right now I feel..." and "Right now I need..."
- Sit quietly for a moment and bring your attention to your whole body. Notice how your toes feel, your feet, your heel and calves. What sensations do you notice in your legs, your groin, your gut and abdomen, your torso and chest, your lungs and heart? What is happening in your shoulders, neck jaw, face and head? You do not need to be able to label or describe these feelings or sensations, just notice and acknowledge them even if you don't know what they are or why they are there.
- Without forcing anything, consider the dominant feeling you experience right now and make a note of it in the first column. If you have a word for it then great, if not then simply describe the sensation or draw a symbol or image.
- As you pay attention to that feeling, consider what need that feeling might be arising as a result of and write that in the second column. Again, trust your gut feel and note down a word a description or a symbol.
- Consider what you can do to satisfy that need, letting your body have an equal role in the decision process. Again, base your answer on your obvious here and now experience.
- Repeat the "feel" and "need" sequence as many times as you can for each sensation you notice.
- Ask yourself the following questions: What did you notice as a result of this experience? What was easy? What was difficult? What did you discover about yourself? How easy was it to notice and then name or describe a feeling? How easy was it to work out what need that feeling arose as a result of?
- Repeat this experiment throughout the day as you experience many different environments and contexts. Pause and pay attention to your body and senses as many times a day as you can, paying attention to what you feel and what you need.

It is impossible to get this experiment wrong – just be curious as to what you notice.

I try to do this experiment as often as possible on a daily basis to help me better attune my bodily sensors so they remain active as a source of information and creative ideas. I also regularly use the two questions in this experiment with groups who I am working with in order to help them become more aware of their entire moment-by-moment, sensuous experience of themselves and others. Doing this regularly avoids the logical brain dominating the agenda. Often in the mists of a meeting where it feels a little stuck, tense, exciting or lively I will ask each person to pause, become more aware 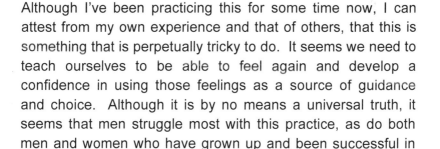 of their whole self and their here-and-now sensual experience and then articulate how they *feel* and what they *need right now*. Nobody is to respond to the answers given, but to simply pay attention to what each person says. Once everyone has done this, the meeting continues but with an extra, deeper layer of awareness of self and others that leads to a marked change in the tone, mood or focus of the interaction. A lot of the time I find that, having done this, the group are more likely to spring to their feet and do something more creative because, all of a sudden, their bodies and senses have arrived and given them clues as to what is needed!

Although I've been practicing this for some time now, I can attest from my own experience and that of others, that this is something that is perpetually tricky to do. It seems we need to teach ourselves to be able to feel again and develop a confidence in using those feelings as a source of guidance and choice. Although it is by no means a universal truth, it seems that men struggle most with this practice, as do both men and women who have grown up and been successful in very masculine cultures, where the language of feelings, sensations and empathy is suppressed or under-developed.

The peril of labels

In my experience, once we learn how to feel and sense again we are immediately faced with another barrier – our compulsion to have to *label* everything. If there are appropriate words to name a feeling then great, but the fact that we can't eloquently label and categorise every sensation we notice doesn't mean that it doesn't exist. I believe that a nonsense word, a noise, a grunt or a gesture is a perfect way of helping others to understand that something is being experienced. Claire Breeze is a friend, co-author of *"The Challenger Spirit: Organisations that disturb the status quo"*[3] and an ordained Buddhist minister. When I was hospitalised and in some considerable pain with an infection in late 2013, she visited me and, through a guided meditation, helped me to become aware of a distinction between the sensations present in my body and the labels that I was placing on them. Through doing this I was able to de-couple my on-going universal description of being in *pain* or *suffering*, instead noticing the texture and movement of my bodily sensations which reduced their intensity  because I related to them in a subtly different, non-logical manner. In this instance, the labels were very unhelpful and letting go of them shifted something important in my present moment awareness of my body.

Turning instinct into action

In his Director's meetings, Keith Johnstone used to ban anyone from talking about things that couldn't just as easily be acted out and experienced. Rather than talking about something that could happen or theoretically debating what *"would happen if..."*, he would insist people got up and tried it out. Having tried something out, rather than just talked about it, the subsequent conversation and actions would be dramatically different as they would come from a position of experience and not theory. This seems to be a good ground rule to adopt in business meetings and organisational change efforts, where a lot of time is spent hypothesizing or talking theoretically and very little trying stuff out. This is not to devalue the power of meaningful conversation – I am merely suggesting that Johnstone's rule might help us differentiate between acting busy versus interacting with each other in a more meaningful and productive way.

The practice of *Embody It* is also about developing this habit of turning our instincts and gut feel into human interaction as quickly as possible, avoiding the evaluation and procrastination that our logical brain insists on. It is about learning to trust our feelings and senses and valuing them as much, if not more, than we do our logical thought. It is about creating a symbiosis between our brain and our body in a way that unleashes our creative spirit through the development of a much wider and richer peripheral awareness.

In late 2013, I spent a week at Schumacher College in Devon in the company of Patricia Shaw, Rob Poynton and a number of other folk who were curious to learn more about Shaw's idea of *Working Live*[4]. I like to think of *Working Live* as the opposite of working dead! It is about being truly present, alive and aware, picking up on the subtle clues, feelings and sensations that are of that moment and choosing to act on them. Working dead is where we have an agenda or a script and doggedly follow it, irrelevant of the fact that something emergent or unplanned requires our immediate attention. The week was an emergent and experimental exploration of what would happen if a group of people simply paid attention to what was going on within themselves, between each other and in relation to the unique location of Schumacher, discovering together what the collaborative work might be, as opposed to having a fixed programme of activities. For me it provided a fascinating insight into the power of paying attention to and improvising with what is on offer versus hypothesising about what could be.

One rule that emerged during the week was that of turning gut feel and impulse into experimentation. Some members of the group soon got very good at turning phrases such as "*I don't know how I would feel if..*" or "*I feel uncomfortable with...*" or "*what if we were to...*" into spontaneous experiments that were neither thought through or subject to any logical design or rationalising. Action arose from noticing a curious feeling and then doing something to make more sense of it. It took a while for us to warm to this new habit as it felt very risky and vulnerable to be so overtly acting on our senses. However, after a while, a fascinating transformation took place where a series of intuitive thoughts, bodily sensations or sensory observations were immediately transformed into embodied experiments – experiments stimulated by impulse as opposed to any well thought-through logic. The result was often confusion, a fog of lost intention and meaning, but each experiment eventually resulted in new insight arising, not through rational conclusions or agreement on theories, but through fully experiencing and acting on sensations live and in the moment.

Trusting our creative bodies

Our bodies, senses and gut instincts continually offer us creative clues and ideas that we don't notice or ignore because we have tuned out of them over the years. Through becoming more aware of them and trusting them we can unleash a rich new vein of creativity into our lives. Once we get good at doing this it helps relieve  some of the pressure we put on our logical brain as we begin to realise that it doesn't need to do all the work. Our bodies are also an express elevator to obviousness! Whilst being clever or original is the role we look to our brain to perform, being obvious is all our bodies can do, so they are pretty good at it. Many times when I have seen people stuck, trying too hard to do something creative I tell them to just relax and do something, anything and the response inevitably starts with a small movement that, if they don't become too self-conscious, turns into a magical piece of writing, a picture, a performance, a key note talk (etc). In rich picture exercises I encourage participants to put their pen on the paper and let their body start to move and see what it turns into as opposed to waiting for their brain to think of what to do or, more typically, tell them that they cannot draw.

Many times I have trusted my body to lead when I've been performing improvisation on stage and have had no idea what to do and, to this day, it has never let me down. Techniques from performance improvisation are wonderful ways of developing our instinctive abilities and tuning into our bodies. One of my favourite exercises that I use with groups in order to develop this ability is a game called *"What are you doing?"* It is very simple in structure and goes something like this: person A performs an action (e.g. digging a hole) and person B asks *"What are you doing?"* Person A then responds by describing an action that is not the one that they are acting out (e.g. *"I'm driving a car"*) *and* person B then performs the action described (i.e. miming driving a car.) The game can be played in pairs or in a big circle and the whole thing continues ad-infinitum until people's heads explode! What is great about this game is that it completely short-circuits the logical brain's habitual role in narrating what the body is doing.

The stretch to this game (that I learnt from Gary Hirsch - www.botjoy.com) is to randomly select two letters of the alphabet to constrain the description. For example, if the two letters are *R* and *T* then all verbal responses to *"What are you doing?"* must start with *R* and *T*, or *T* and *R*. (*"I'm rotating turnips"*, *"I'm tuning Ronald"*, *"I'm translating rudely"* for example). I was recently working with a group who were  playing this game with the tricky letters *U* and *W*. It came to the turn of a very nervous man who could not think of anything to say when he was asked *"What are you doing?"* His face went red, his brain was in overdrive and he murmured, muttered and squirmed for at least 15 seconds. I then suggested he took a look at what clues his body was giving him. He looked down and noticed that his hands had changed their movement and now looked like they were cleaning something smooth and round. *"I'm washing up!"* he exclaimed, proudly realising that, whilst he was mentally struggling to be creative, his body had already done the work for him – he simply had to notice it.

Summary: Embody It

This practice is about becoming more aware of the role our bodies and senses play in nurturing our creative spirit. It is about becoming more attuned to the creative signals, clues and cues that they are continually giving as.   It is about striking a more symbiotic partnership between brain and body, between logic and gut feel and between thought and feeling. It is about learning to separate sensation from description and letting go of our need to label and eloquently explain something to legitimise its existence. It is about jumping up and doing stuff based on no more than an instinct or sensation as acting on our sensuous experience is an express elevator to being obvious. Through continual practice we often find that we are rarely left not knowing what to do as we always have a plethora of creative offers being made from places within us that we have often ignored.

Embody it	
Let go	• Dominance of logical thought. • Taboo of our bodies and senses in the workplace. • The need to explain everything with words in order for it to be valid.
Be more	• Pause, tune in and notice. • Treat every sensation as an *offer*. • Separate sensation from description/label.
Experiment by	• Acting on impulse. • Doing stuff rather than talking about doing it. • Seeing the world as a sensual experience as opposed to a logical, mechanistic one.

Chapter 8 References

[1] Christopher Bergland (2007) "*The Athlete's Way: Sweat and the Biology of Bliss.*" St Martin's Press

[2] Mihaly Csikszentmihalyi, M. (2002) *Flow: The classic work on how to achieve happiness.* USA: Random House

[3] Khurshed Denhugara & Claire Genkai Breeze (2011) "*The Challenger Spirit: Organisations that Disturb the Status Quo.*" London:LID Publishing

[4] Patricia Shaw & Ralph Stacey [Eds] (2006) "*Experiencing Risk, Spontaneity and Improvisation in Organisational Change: Working Live.*" Oxford: Routledge

Chapter 9 Make Others Look Good
Championing the creative spirit of others

"Improvisation is an expression of good nature."
                                                    Keith Johnstone

I once worked with an executive
whose first job in life was as a
policeman in the Singaporean police
force. He told me many stories of the
robust training that they were put
through in order to build trust
between the cadets. He told of

challenging physical and mental exercises including having to
leap blindfolded from a helicopter that was only flying at
around three feet off the ground, but had just descended from
300 feet, with the order to jump coming from a colleague when
it was at a safe enough height - an ultimate exercise in trust.

The story that I most regularly recall is one of how he was
trained to handle riots. I remember him telling me that, when
facing a marauding crowd of rioters, the group were trained to
stand back-to-back in a circle and the only rule was that *"the
person on your left's life is more important than your
own."* This meant that, in the heat of the moment, they were
totally present, inter-connected and supporting each another
because of this simple rule. Nobody was looking out for
themselves because they knew somebody else was looking
out for them. Nobody was operating as an individual because
their awareness was focused on others. He took this rule as a
core principle to the teams he worked with in the corporate
world and was regarded as an exceptional leader to work for
in a number of organisations.

The practice of Making Others Look Good is similar in principle to Singaporean riot control and, although not as dangerous, can be surprisingly difficult to master. It is one thing to begin to nurture one's own creative spirit but another to support and champion the development of others. This is essentially what this practice is about. It is about putting the majority of our attention and effort on making the creative spirit of others shine without thought of our own self-image. It is about helping others to reduce the anxiety that their newly emerging creative self may cause. It is about giving others a good time by paying particular attention to their creative needs at any point in time and helping them be fulfilled. It is about helping others become more comfortable with being mad, bad and wrong, saying "yes" (to the mess), being obvious, being altered, failing happy and trusting their bodies and senses. It is about getting into the mindset that the *person on the left's* creativity is more important that your own. The symbiosis this creates builds the incredible trust, energy and commitment required to nurture a community and culture that deeply values imagination, creativity, improvisation and play.

This practice is a little more difficult to intuitively grasp than the others as it is 100% inter-personal and slightly paradoxical in nature. People often ask *"So I'm to focus on my here-and-now awareness of myself and how the practices show up for me AND at the same time put my efforts into the creative development of others?"* The simple (but possibly unhelpful) answer to this question is *"Yes!"* If we want others to join us on our Creative Adventures we have to experiment with how to work within this paradox.

I always begin my creativity and innovation workshops with at least an hour of warm-up/let go exercises. I use these exercises to begin to short-circuit the habitual social norms, beliefs, behaviours and assumptions of the groups I am working with. An essential exercise I use is the improvisation game *Eight Things*. *Eight Things* involves groups of around six to eight people arranging themselves in a circle and one person stepping into the middle. Somebody from the surrounding circle calls out a category and the person in the middle has to name eight things from that category as quickly as possible, trying to minimise hesitation and logical thought. As each item in the category is named, the people on the outside of the circle loudly and enthusiastically count the things and when a total of eight is reached they whoop and applaud wildly before the next person steps in and the process is repeated.

Whilst this is a great exercise for freeing up our spontaneous thought and dampening our fear of being perceived as mad, bad and wrong, the main reason I insist on doing it is because it makes the person in the middle look good. No matter what they say, what they do, how much they struggle or shine, the group on the outside loves and applauds their contribution, which is incredibly affirming and confidence building. Even though it is a game, at a deep psychological level this experience seems to shift something and make new connections.

A recent example of this exercise in an innovation workshop unfolded as follows:

'M' stepped into the middle. Somebody from the group shouted out *dogs* as the category and the exercise began.

M: Poodle
Group: One! [Said enthusiastically. The entire group are smiling and leaning in towards M]
M: Labrador
Group: Two!
M: Er - Dalmatian
Group: Three!
M: [Brief pause] er- a Daschund
Group: Four!
M: A Sausage Dog
Group: Five!
M: A...p...Pretzel....dog
Group: Six
M: A grey dog
Group: Seven
M: A blue dog
Group: Eight! Yaaaaay! [Group wildly applauds M]

'M' left the circle flushed, but feeling affirmed and happy. The group didn't pedantically point out that a Dachshund and a Sausage Dog are essentially the same thing, nor did they point out that a Pretzel Dog doesn't exist, nor did they treat the suggestion of a grey or a blue dog as cheating – they simply supported whatever came out of 'M''s mouth. Even if the person in the middle of the circle says "*I don't know*", expresses an elongated "*errrrrrr*", repeats a previous suggestion or makes a confused noise, the group will applaud and count it as a valid contribution anyway. This is an exercise in making others look good and people often tell me that it was this experience that helped them feel safe enough to contribute wild and crazy ideas later in the day.

A fledgling creative spirit is very fragile and it only takes one or two negative knocks to cause it to retreat back into the depths of our subconscious, making it even harder to coax back out. Matt Kingdom, founder of the innovation company !What If?, describes the mutual support required here in a typically of-the-wall metaphorical way: *"It only takes one person to poo in the pool. After that nobody wants to get in, even if the poo is subsequently removed!"[1]*

Experiment: Spotting poos in the pool

- *Set yourself a period of time for this experiment. It could be a specific meeting or workshop, a particular conversation or a time period such as a day or a week.*
- *For the period you have chosen, try to become deeply aware of the emerging creative spirit of others. Where do you spot others taking creative risks, volunteering new ideas, challenging norms and habits and where do you notice yourself or others squashing these new behaviours?*
- *Try to spot others being mad, bad and wrong, saying "yes" (to the mess), being obvious, being altered, failing happy and using their senses and intuition to spontaneously guide their actions. When you spot them doing this, publicly acknowledge and praise these behaviours even if you feel it makes you loose face, status or credibility.*
- *Reflect on the following questions: What did you notice in others? Where did you see these practices flourish in others? Where did you see them being suppressed? How easy was it to publicly acknowledge and praise these practices? How did you feel when you did this? If you didn't publicly acknowledge and praise them why didn't you? What might all of this tell you about yourself and the culture you work in?*

It is impossible to get this experiment wrong – just be curious as to what you notice.

Permission

If I were to boil the core principles of this book down into one word it would be *permission*. Expanding the individual and social *permission field* (i.e. what is acceptable around here) is essential in allowing our collective creative spirits to develop. Initially, we have to find ways of giving ourselves permission to develop these practices and, once we have done so, we require a broader social permission to develop them further and give us the confidence to allow our creative spirit to shine in front of others. Even the most passionate emerging creative spirit can easily get crushed if the culture around it suffocates and stifles it enough. In other words, putting a clean creative fish back into dirty water results in a dirty fish! In my experience, the trust and mutual understanding required between individuals, groups and their surrounding culture to nurture creativity is the biggest challenge in applying this work at an organisational level. A standoff of Wild-West proportions can emerge where nobody wants to show their own creative spirit first because they feel it may be criticised or mocked by others ("*You show me yours before I show you mine!*").

This practice is about helping to bring movement to this stuck cultural pattern and it begins with those of us who are further along the creative journey bravely showing a little more of our own creative spirit in order to give permission for others to show theirs. If they do, it is our role to wildly support its growth, even if we lose face through doing so. In this sense this practice is less about ourselves and more about others.

Tong Len is the Buddhist practice of giving and taking – a practice which helps us to develop a deeper awareness of how much of our focus is on self and how much is on others.

 The Dalai Lama explains *"We tend to relate to this so-called 'self' as a precious core at the centre of our being, something that is really worth taking care of, to the extent that we are willing to overlook the well-being of others. In contrast, our attitude towards others often resembles indifference; at best we may have some concern for them, but even this may simply remain at the level of a feeling or an emotion."* He continues *"...the point of this particular practice is to reverse this attitude so that we reduce the intensity of our grasping and the attachment we have to ourselves and endeavour to consider the well-being of others as significant and important."*[2] Making Others Look Good is about acts of creative *tong len* and using ourselves as a catalyst for widening the permission field for others.

I recently worked with a group of Learning and Development professionals from the Higher Education sector and we spent a few hours undertaking exercises that gradually widened the group's permission field in order to unleash their creative talents. This group were so good at making each other look good and supporting spontaneous and imaginative thought that, at the end of the session, many of them were amazed at what they had said and done. One participant, a lady in her late 50's, exclaimed with a big smile on her face *"I can't believe what I've been saying and doing today. None of it seemed to come from the me I know! I'm a little freaked out. What have you all done to me?"*

Experiment: Excavating cultural permission fields

- *Think of a particular environment in which you feel it is important to develop a culture of creativity. This could be a company, a department, a club, a social group, a family (etc.)*
- *On a piece of paper, draw six big boxes and above each one write the name of one of the six creative practices: Mad, Bad & Wrong, Say "yes" (to the mess), Be Obvious-Be Altered, Fail Happy, Embody It and Make Others Look Good.*
- *Divide each box into two. Label one half as "culturally acceptable" and the other half as "culturally unacceptable"*

- *For each practice, consider what is culturally acceptable - what do you feel people have permission to do without being reprimanded or rejected? For example: what can people say "yes" to and still be culturally accepted, how mad, bad or wrong can people be without being culturally rejected? Add your notes to the relevant box.*
- *For each practice, consider what is culturally unacceptable - what would it take for people to overstep the mark and step outside of the cultural norms? For example: what would it take for somebody to be too obvious, to listen to their feelings too much etc? Add your notes to the relevant box.*
- *Reflect on your diagram and see what you notice. What seems to be the most underdeveloped practice? What is the most mature practice? What is a simple experiment you can undertake to support the development of one or all practices in others? What can you do to lead the way in this experimental process and give others permission? What would prevent you from doing this? What does this tell you about the culture?*

It is impossible to get this experiment wrong – just be curious as to what you notice.

Becoming the creative face on the dartboard

In their book *"The Challenger Spirit: Organisations that Disturb the Status Quo"*[3], Claire Breeze and Khurshed Denhugara describe a quality that challenger-leaders exhibit that they call *"being the face on the dartboard."*  Being the face on the dartboard is about being willing and able to publicly stand for something that is important to you, but may make you unpopular with others as it is a strong challenge to the status quo. The most important thing about being the face on the dartboard is being able robustly challenge in a way that does not exhaust and psychologically damage oneself in the process. This is an important point for corporate Creative Adventurers to be continually aware of. Cultures that are dominated by mechanistic, logical and deductive thinking, or individuals who obsessively cling to safe-certainty are often highly intolerant of novelty and creativity. Even organisations that state they want more creativity and innovation may end up stifling it or even punishing it when it begins to emerge in ways they did not anticipate, or when it challenges some of the deeply ingrained cultural norms.

Making Others Look Good is about spotting individuals who are bravely trying to bring their own creative spirit into their work for the good of their organisation and publicly supporting them even though it may result in us becoming unpopular. But, as Breeze and Denhugara suggest, this requires us to develop a significant amount of personal resilience in order to maintain energy for our own Creative Adventure. This is why it is so important to continue developing our own practice in parallel and to seek out and connect with other adventurers who can support our own wellbeing.

Summary: Make Others Look Good

This practice is about letting go of the importance of our own self image in service of nurturing the creative spirit of others. It is about becoming more aware of the small, spontaneous, creative signs that others exhibit and becoming deeply appreciative of the bravery it might have taken them to experiment publicly. It is about metaphorically believing that the *person on your left's* creative spirit is more important than your own and using yourself as an instrument to give permission to others, irrelevant of how much hierarchical or influential power you have or are confronted with. It is about tuning into and scanning the surrounding culture, noticing and naming where it is supportive or intolerant of a creative spirit. It is about being an activist in stimulating a creative social movement within a culture you are deeply passionate about, even if it involves periods of being the creative face on the dartboard.

Make Others Look Good	
Let go	• Obsessively striving to preserve self image. • Conforming with the cultural status quo (be that consciously or unconsciously.) • *Pooing in the pool* and letting others get away with doing so.
Be more	• Supportive of the emerging creative spirit of others and publicly acknowledging and praising these practices in others. • Creative *tong len* – balancing giving and taking of creative spirit. • The creative face on the dartboard.
Experiment by	• Being bolder and more overt with one's own creative spirit in order to give permission to others to do the same. • Recognising and rewarding others for experimenting and showing their own creative spirit in public. • Finding partners and support groups for covert and overt Creative Adventures.

Chapter 9 References

1 Matt Kingdom speaking at !WhatIf? "*Top Dog*" event in London, November 2008

2 Dalai Lama (2000) "*The Dalai Lama's Book of Transformation.*" London:Thornsons

3 Khurshed Denhugara & Claire Genkai Breeze (2011) "*The Challenger Spirit: Organisations that Disturb the Status Quo*" London:LID Publishing

PART THREE

CREATIVE ADVENTURES

Chapter 10 Ordinary Stories of Adventure

"There's nothing as practical as good theory."
Kurt Lewin (1890-1947)

I felt very anxious as I sat on the train en-route to the storytelling workshop. I've come to think that a healthy level of anxiety in my work is a positive sign that I'm taking it seriously - a kind of anxiety that a mentor of mine calls "unsupported excitement" which is an overall positive thing. This anxiety was different though. I was genuinely worried that things would go terribly wrong. I'd never collaborated with the consultant I was working with and, whilst I'd initially been OK with the idea of us experimenting by working together, my feelings had changed when I discovered that the client was from an organisation who are a long standing and much cherished client of mine! If this all went terribly wrong what would they think of me? Would they decide to scrap the other work I had planned with them? I'd never worked with this guy before, I'd met him once and got on really well so I'd just said "yes" to his offer. We'd only designed the session over the phone and now, as I thought about it, I could only see where things could go wrong. My heart pounded and my brain burnt. What could I do? I sat for a moment and looked out of the window as Battersea Power station flew past in a blur indicating I would soon have to disembark at Waterloo. "Practice what you preach you idiot!" a voice in my head suddenly exclaimed. I thought for a moment and then reached into my bag and pulled out my

Creative Practice die[1]. I rolled it on the seat next to me. It tumbled briefly, stopped and the words Fail Happy stared back at me. A smile spread across my face, my heartbeat reduced and I realised that whatever happened would be just fine.

This story is vividly etched in my memory. It happened about halfway through writing this book, at a time where I was totally immersed in articulating what the six creative practices were all about. I was giving numerous conference talks about them, writing blogs about them and I had began to bring them into my one-to-one coaching to help others begin their own Creative Adventures. In other words, I was so immersed in *talking* about them that I'd stopped *doing* them. I'd slipped from an on-going embodied practice, into an alternate reality of theory and hypothesis. It took my own intense fear of failure at the storytelling workshop to remind me that taking one's own medicine is often a difficult thing!

My hope is that everything so far in this book is simple, appealing and somewhat challenging but overall makes sense. However, there is a difference between intellectually getting the idea of turning our lives and careers into Creative Adventures, versus taking the plunge and truly experiencing them. Playing with the experiments in the book is a good start point but we only really begin our adventures properly when we take the first tentative steps out of theory and into the messy practice of blending them into our day-to-day lives. In this instance, the difference between theory and practice is as stark as the difference between looking at a photo of a beautiful Pacific island and physically going there to experience it.

Turning theory into practice – some short stories

Irrelevant of who we are, what we do and what labels we place on ourselves, we are all human beings and have the same amount of creative potential within us. As Dr Seuss concludes in *"Horton Hears a Who"* [2], *"...a person's a person no matter how small"* and anyone can turn their life or career into a Creative Adventure simply through nurturing a deep passion to bring more liveliness and excitement into their work.

Whilst Part II of this book gives us an idea of how we might experiment using some simple practices, there is no more of a compelling call to action than hearing the stories of others who have already began. Rather than end the book with a list of things that you should now go and do (I'd prefer to leave it up to you to decide what your next steps are), this chapter shares some stories from normal, everyday people I know or I have worked with, who have chosen to try to bring more imagination, creativity, improvisation, play and adventure into their lives or into the lives of others. Their stories may be big, small, work related or just things that happened in their personal lives. They have chosen to share their stories in the hope that they will give you ideas of how to begin your own Creative Adventure.

A handful of their short stories of ordinary adventure now follow.

Ola Odumosu – The Yes Lady

Ola is an Organisation Development (OD) and Diversity and Inclusion consultant who runs her own business called New Chapter.  She decided to go out on her own because she wanted more freedom, fun and self-expression in her work, but had recently realised how straight and predictable it had become. Having noticed this, she decided to try to re-connect with her original motivation for running her own business and experiment by saying "yes" more to the scary opportunities and offers that came her way.

I previously worked in a big corporate, which was great, but everything seemed so serious! I stepped out on my own because I wanted to create something that struck a better balance between 'serious' and 'playful.' However, what I ended up doing was some great pieces of work, but in a very straight, logical way. My background is scientific and I realised that I had unconsciously defaulted to what was safe for me, instead of experimenting by bringing in more of my own creative spirit. My business was going well, but I felt like there was something missing, something I was holding back and something in me that I hadn't let free yet. I realised that I was only saying "yes" to things that were in my comfort zone, or holding back and not saying "yes" until something felt less scary and I was missing a lot of great opportunities as a result. I was holding back because I didn't think I would get them right or achieve perfection. I decided that, if I was going to achieve my original aim, I needed to say "yes" more to things that were scary or things that I didn't think would work or get me anywhere near perfection. The very act of saying "yes" to this commitment felt scary.

The first "yes" challenge didn't take long to come about, as a large multinational organisation invited me to become part of a high-profile OD faculty. In order to become part of the faculty, I would have to take part in a full-on assessment day: do a presentation, a case study exercise, give a talk to the board, be interviewed (etc). This is not only something that I would normally say "no" to, but something I would actively avoid! I said "yes" and then immediately thought to myself "What have I just done?" I had about five weeks until the assessment day and I kept thinking to myself "How can I get out of this?" Loads of other stuff was going on in my life at that time so I had many genuine excuses to back out and say "no". However, I stuck with my yes, went along to the assessment and was accepted onto the faculty! What I learnt from this experience was that the initial yes isn't necessarily the hardest bit, it is sticking to that yes when things get tough. I'm starting to realise that saying "yes" is actually me giving my word that I will do something, so it isn't OK to then back out of it. Realising this helps me maintain a resilient yes.

Another example of this was a singing musical improvisation workshop that I said "yes" to, even though it sounded absolutely terrifying. As soon as I'd said "yes" I started to think of a load of genuinely good reasons as to why I wouldn't be able to make it. However, I managed to hold myself in this uncomfortable yes for long enough to make it to the workshop and I had an amazing experience.

The more I have leant into the difficult yes, the easier it has become. I said "yes" to running a challenging workshop for

200 graduates, I said "yes" to travelling to Angola and Australia in the same week and, most recently, I said "yes" to running a Diversity and Inclusion workshop for a unique and very high profile organisation who have a reputation for being rather quirky and risqué. *The organisation wanted me to help them design and facilitate a workshop for a cohort of their women's mentoring programme, with the objective of helping them to celebrate its ending and work out what to do next to make sure their great work continued to live on. I decided that this was an ideal, but high-risk, opportunity to play with striking a better balance between the polarities of freedom, creativity, structure and logic that I hadn't yet managed to achieve. I wrote a great proposal for them that I was very proud of, but when I sat down to talk them through it, I could see in their faces that it wasn't what they wanted! This was really difficult as I was so proud of what I had written. I had put lots of colour and visuals in it but, whilst they liked some of the logical and systemic thinking it provoked, they thought it was far too straight and not creative enough! I asked them what more they wanted and they said that it must have structure but also be able to evolve in the moment, it must have impact but it has to be safe, it must be high energy but mustn't turn people off, it must have flare but not scare people, it must be modelled by me but I mustn't lead the participants. It sounded an impossible request! I remember leaving, not having a clue what to do.*

I was stuck but I decided to ask myself what would be the most obvious thing to do and what came to mind, out of nowhere, was my passion for stories and storytelling. I realised that stories have structure but can evolve, stories have impact but are safe, stories can have high energy and flare without turning people off or scaring them and I could tell a story without leading the participants to any particular conclusion. My experiment was born and I decided that, if I was going to fail, I would aim to do so spectacularly! I designed some simple and some risky story telling exercises, I brought in lots of different visuals, I even brought in my story-telling sticks that I'd bought in Australia and decided that I would just try to have fun with all these different creative elements. The more I decided it was OK to fail happy, the more I experimented. The more I said "yes" to the mess and being OK with not knowing exactly what was going to happen, the more I relaxed into it. The result was a workshop that created an environment of safe uncertainty – the room layout and my high-level design bringing just enough structure to make it feel safe but allowing enough flexibility for everything else to evolve and happen in-the-moment. It was such a success. The participants were so open in their story sharing that it allowed us to talk openly about what had happened in the past and the wisdom that those past experiences had brought to life. They were able to tell stories of their future legacy, the patterns of relationships that they wanted to create and some simple, guiding rules to live by in order to create them.

Saying "yes" to failing happy gave me permission to throw all of my ideas together, integrating different experiences, theories and models in a creative way that ended up becoming a unique experiment. It was like giving in to the idea of failing happy allowed me to get into a state of flow in which, ironically, I didn't fail. I realised that fear is something that makes me say "no" or makes me say "yes" and then find excuses to back out of it. I learnt from the experiences of the OD faculty assessment, the musical improv session and the Diversity and Inclusion workshop, that the actual experience is

never as bad as the anticipated experience. The anticipated experience tends to be that it will be continuously, horrible and scary throughout, but the actual experience is very different, with a few mildly scary moments but also many moments of fun, joy and discovery.

Amelia Morris – Inspiration in the dentist's chair

Amelia Morris is a Leadership Development professional for a large multi-national telecommunications company. She became curious as to what she would discover by experimenting in her work and personal life.

I have always been rather introverted, however stages in my life, such as my gap year and my first two years at university ensured I became a more confident person. It was not until I began working at my placement job that I realised I still had some of these traits, such as being a people-pleaser and being desperately petrified of sounding stupid in front of peers and even friends. It was only when I started to become deeply curious about the practice of Mad, Bad and Wrong that I had that "eureka!" moment where I realised that I shouldn't actually care about what other people think of me as much as I do...or did. I began by simply trying to think less about the consequences of something stupid I might blurt out and more about the opportunities I had already missed so far in my career, especially considering I work in a culture that encourages questions and creativity.

From this point on, creativity almost started coming naturally to me in every form I could have expected. I recall one day going to the dentist, an impossibly boring annual routine, but it was here I had my first idea that I didn't suppress because I considered it impossible or idiotic. My dentist was doing the routine checks such as whether or not I was a smoker, to which I replied "no". I started to think about the damage that smokers must do to their teeth and began to let my mind wander with no limits, saying "yes" to what ever came to me in that moment. I came out of my appointment believing that there could be some kind of toothpaste that would be used once in the morning and once in the evening, but would have some kind of ingredient that makes all cigarettes taste foul, enabling people to quit very easily. I do not know if this is plausible or possible, but I noticed that it was the first time I let my creativity take its course without destroying it mid-flow and it is an idea that I am going to pursue somehow.

Since the dentist chair moment, I have been inventing multi-million pound ideas in my head, some of which could even be possible! The practice of Mad, Bad and Wrong has significantly reduced my fear of being mocked or shut down, which I not only carry with me at work, but also in my personal life. It has changed the way I view not only my own ideas, but also other peoples' ideas. I now believe there is no such thing as a crazy or wrong idea - everything can be worked on.

It is never easy to express potentially laughable ideas to colleagues or friends especially if, as in my case, it involves letting go of our social anxiety. However I think it is imperative to remind yourself that very little happens right first time. Is there really any successful innovative idea that did not have to be altered and re-tested? So what makes us believe that we are expected to get it right first time? Any idea is a good idea – or perhaps more accurately, good can come from any idea. So yes, ideas may be killed far too quickly or deemed *hopeless in this world, but that should not prevent innovation, even if it means creating 1000 unusable light bulbs!*

Stuart Harrison – Inexpert museum tour guide

Stuart is Senior Vice President of Finance for a global blue chip organisation. He is also a *Creative Adventures* coaching client of mine. *Creative Adventures* are one-to-one experiences where I help individuals discover the edge of their comfort zone, make friends  with it and learn from it in unusual, experiential ways. Stuart wanted to work on being more in-the-moment and present with others, letting go of his need for control and having to plan everything in advance. I designed him an adventure in which he was suddenly asked to give a spontaneous guided tour of the Victoria and Albert Museum in London to a complete stranger. He had no idea what was in store for him other than an instruction to meet at South Kensington tube station at a certain time. He recounts the story of his experience.

I went through an interesting cycle that day. I started by feeling quite cool and relaxed about the whole thing and my rational head was saying "it will be an interesting experience" and that we wouldn't be doing it if there wasn't a purpose to it. I then got out of the out of the tube at South Kensington and said to myself "Oh God!" I began feeling tense as I wondered what it was all going to be about – the unknown. I knew in my head it would be OK because you [Steve] were doing it, which made it feel safe enough, but I still felt nervous and apprehensive as to exactly what the adventure was going to be. One of the tensest experiences was seeing the envelope with the details of the adventure inside and not knowing what was in it. It felt like that moment just before the exam paper arrives!

When I opened the envelope and read the instructions, my nervousness turned into curiosity and I thought that, as long as I don't make a complete and utter idiot of myself in the public domain of the museum, it was actually quite an interesting challenge. I really liked the idea of having to do something where all I could do was go-with-the-flow. This was exciting, as I would normally prefer to have time to plan.

After we met James, [the pre-arranged stranger] we immediately walked into the body sculpture room and I was confronted with a statue of a naked woman! That threw me for two reasons: 1) It was the first thing we came across and all of a sudden the reality of what I had to do hit me and 2) I was worried that, if I trusted my spontaneous-self I might end up saying something politically incorrect!

However, once we got out of the sculpture room and into the central part of the museum I started to make connections between exhibits and all of a sudden I realised that doing this was helping me to improvise. By making connections between the obvious things around me, I suddenly felt like I was talking creatively and not just babbling. This is important to me as I want to be passionate about something but want to do it in a coherent way. In the next room, there were a number of brightly coloured vases and I was inspired by the different colours and shapes of glass and became curious as to what they meant. I found it easy to improvise, as the things

I was looking at inspired me and I was able to be present and obvious in talking about them, rather than thinking ahead.

However, when got into the main Architecture gallery that James had requested we visited, my mind-set changed. I think I suddenly perceived that the main task had began and I started to go into my head a bit more and I was conscious that I needed to keep talking. I also realised that, although I was interested in the architecture, it didn't inspire me. This also pushed me back into logical mode and I started to plan ahead a thread that would connect the exhibits. Why did I do that? I think it gave me a certain comfort-level and made the task easier. On reflection, I do think that I was creative but, on the other hand, I realise I was not as creative as I could have been had I just gone with whatever came into my head.

The main insight I took away from this adventure was realising how everyday things around me have the potential to inspire me and how being inspired helps me to be present, go-with-the-flow and improvise. I'm curious about the difference between inspiration and preparation. I got a thrill from going with the flow because I felt inspired. However, if I'd been given time to prepare in advance (which I would normally prefer) the whole thing would have been a lot more boring! My personality is more about being in control and maybe that's why I like to prepare so much. In the scenario you [Steve] put me through, I couldn't be in control and I felt a certain freedom to just be creative. I felt liberated because it was OK to say what came into my head. Spontaneity and letting go of control feels quite important for me as I strive become a more motivational leader. I can't be motivational if I'm not inspired and loosened up enough to be spontaneous.

Gary Aldam – A creative coming-of-age

Gary Aldam is a Business Change and Performance Consultant for a large multi-national pharmaceutical company. He spends a lot of his time facilitating workshops and meetings with senior leaders and decided to experiment with the practices as part of his day-to-day work.

Recently, I've been trying to consciously do some experiments with a number of senior leadership teams, as well as with individual leaders that I coach. I made a conscious decision to experiment with Mad, Bad and Wrong because of the perceived seniority of those I was working with. I decided to tell myself that, essentially it doesn't really matter, these are just human beings who are interested in what I have to say and, whilst they may perceive it as being odd, it may also shift the needle somewhat. In doing this I came to realise something – I'm in my 50's now! Career-wise I'm looking at retirement soon so, even if it does go pear-shaped, what am I going to lose? I think sometimes I'm still habitually thinking like I was 20-25 years ago! Now I catch myself and say "I don't need to worry about this anymore. I'm old!" In the past I realise that this got in my way – worrying too much about what people would think about me that might affect my career path. I've been able to completely drop this now and the outcomes from some of my experiments have been really interesting.

I'm saying "yes" more and biting the bullet, doing things that I'd normally put off because I'm not sure what is going to happen. For example, I've recently started inviting myself to a number of leadership meetings where I need to influence the team and they've said "yes" and the meetings have gone very well. I now wonder what I was so hung up about in the past. By doing it I've realised that the bad scenarios I imagined simply weren't true!

I was presenting to a senior leadership team last week and I went into it with a Fail Happy and Mad, Bad and Wrong perspective in my mind and was really challenging to them. I had one of those 'Alan Sugar' moments, where the leader of the group was saying one thing and I was challenging him with something else. Despite being more confident in myself I still came out of the session wondering whether I had wound him up too much. However, the next day, everywhere I went, people were coming up to me and saying "What you did yesterday has really rattled some cages", "We've talked about what you said further at subsequent meetings", "That really got them thinking", "On the back of last week we've decided to change our key business lead and lag measures" and I said to myself "Wow!" Had I gone in in a really safe, compliant way and presented my scripted presentation it would never have had the same effect. I realise that Mad, Bad & Wrong isn't about being horrible to somebody, it is just about being honest, being obvious and just saying it how it is. In this particular instance it has ended up with making the senior leaders look good. Realising this has been very liberating for me. I've consciously gone into situations thinking failure doesn't matter in so much as, if I fail, I'm not going to beat myself up about it. What I've found is that, although I've gone in with that attitude, I rarely fail and actually end up with some successes I never thought I could get away with! However, over time I seem to forget how great those successes were and the fear barrier builds back up again, so I think it is important to practice on a constant basis as it is easy to fall back into saying "no".

Jennifer Lopez – Failing Happy

Jennifer is a Vice President of Corporate Support at an American banking organistaion and a student of the Case Western University Masters in Positive Organisational Change Programme. She recently spent some

time with me at Ashridge Business School, where I facilitated an immersive experience of the Creative Practices for the Case Western students. Jennifer reflects on her experience.

Before I came to Ashridge, I participated in a simulation exercise where I volunteered to be the CEO. I failed miserably. By the time we made it to Ashridge for our workshops, my heart had gone through a lot of emotions. I cried because of how I let my colleagues down. I felt the need to defend myself and quickly recognised I really couldn't. I was afraid I was going to lose my friendships. I felt humiliated. I knew that the simulation could have gone either way but I wanted it to be successful. I also knew that, no matter what the outcome would be, I just needed to do it anyway. I needed to get to know what I was afraid of and it felt pretty safe to do it in a simulation. I didn't realise the intensity that would come from the exercise though, in particular hearing others express themselves about how I performed in the role of CEO. I had to listen and accept the responsibility for the ways in which I could have done better, the way in which others felt about my interactions with them and the ways in which I just simply failed. When we got to Ashridge I felt even more open to what I would learn and when the words Fail Happy appeared on the wall, I felt tears come to my eyes. I had failed miserably in front of my colleagues in many ways just a few days earlier, but now I was able to realise that the risk was worth taking because I had actually failed happy. However, I did not have a huge smile on my face and say, "Wow, that was so great! Did you see how I screwed that up, hurt your feelings and made a mess of things! Woo!!!"

No, my failing happy was different. I was happy because I took a risk in front of my class, not really knowing the outcome. I was happy because I learned really important lessons. I was happy because I had a great opportunity to listen to how people felt about the experience. I failed happy because I needed to grow. I failed happy because I was the recipient of an amazing experience, watching people's emotions, listening to their questions and knowing what it feels like to really have to own when you just don't know what to do. It is one thing to talk about the concept of failing happy but it is only through experiencing it and taking the time to make sense of it, even through a simulation, that you really begin to get what it is all about.

Katy Bateson – Mad, Bad and Wrong dinner conversations

Katy Bateson is an NHS administrator and a talented improvisation teacher/ performer who has single-handedly brought this creative practice to the UK city of Lancaster. She rolled the Creative Practice die[1] just before going to a friend's dinner party and it landed on *Mad, Bad & Wrong.* Katy explains what happened.

I had forgotten consciously about the dice roll when I went to my friend's house for tea, but I think it had lodged in my subconscious somehow. There were three of us there in total and we got onto the topic of religion and the justice system and my friends were having an enthusiastic, friendly debate about it. Normally I avoid any kind of conflict at all cost. Even if the conflict is minor or doesn't involve me I still find myself shying away to the point where I will leave the room. But on this occasion I decided to join in. I vocalised my opinions, even if they were the opposite of others and gave reasons as to why I disagreed. It felt very liberating to express my opinion when I normally would hold back to avoid conflict or upsetting anyone. What surprised me was that nobody reacted in the extreme way that I had worried they would, in fact they seemed to appreciate my perspective. I felt very proud of myself because I had done something I wouldn't normally do. The big learning for me was that I can vocalise my thoughts and opinions, even if they differ to other people, without causing upset. I concluded that I can afford to be a little bit more mad, bad and wrong that I'd previously thought.

John Paul Flintoff – Daring to do

John Paul Flintoff is a journalist, author and a coach. He has been training in improvisation for a number of years now and has been experimenting with many of the ideas of Keith Johnstone that have influenced this book. He told me about his experience of beginning to let his creative spirit emerge through experimenting with these practices.

I've had so many ideas and got so excited about things that, in the past, I would have kept to myself and not dared to even name as things I'm interested in. Now when I say that I'm going to do them I expect everyone to stop and point, but everyone actually reacts positively. Fear is closely related to this idea of failing happy and I tell this enough to other people that I've internalised it for myself. If things don't work out the way I want them to work out then that's actually alright. It's not the end of the world. I now strongly believe that if there isn't a chance of something not working out, it's really not worth doing otherwise you're just being a zombie – leading a life of total guaranteed outcomes and that's not a life. I don't want to be undead! I want to have that delicious experience of failure as a possibility.

I'm not saying failure itself is enjoyable, I really don't like failure and there are some areas where I'm quite happy at failing but some areas where I am not. For example, I was recently on the tube with my daughter and ended up getting into a slightly bickering argument and subsequently thought "Oh God! I've failed unhappily here". Failure is troubling and painful and it hurts, but having a daughter is only worth it if

that's a possibility otherwise I'm just in some crazy fantasy that's not real. I just have to continually remind myself that it's OK to fail happy.

Saying "yes" to imperfection is also key – if you don't accept the possibility of failure, you won't even start because you are so in love with the perfect thing that you are imagining. I find this when I teach people to draw and they say they can't. It is kind of an inverted pride - they seem to want to become the best artist in the room and if they can't achieve that then they don't want to try anything. Are they really saying that they can't draw? If they are then why not just do a crap drawing and prove it! People can draw if they get rid of their own referee because nobody else really minds that much how good they are.

I started to draw my own inner critic, with speech bubbles telling me things like "you're not ready!" I thought this was a terrible, shameful secret of mine and, if I ever let anyone see it, they would see through me and I'd be rumbled! Then I experimented by showing these drawings to whole classes in order to get them to do it for themselves. Surprisingly, I noticed by their faces, that they were slightly bored and uninterested! They didn't care about my little voices as they were already wondering what the nagging voices in their own heads were!

Dominic Fitch – Celebrating process, not performance

Dom is Creative Director at Shakespeare Schools Festival (www.ssf.uk.com), a charitable organisation that nurtures the creativity and confidence of young people (aged eight to 18) by helping them and their  teachers put on unique, abridged versions of Shakespeare plays in professional theatres. SSF works with secondary, primary and special schools all over the UK, but specifically targets disadvantaged schools. Dom shared some stories with me about the key philosophies of SSF, some of the challenges pupils and teachers face stepping onto the stage and emphasised the importance of celebrating process and not just performance when looking to nurture the creative spirit of young people and their teachers.

We work with children in professional theatre venues around the country (e.g. the 700 seater West Yorkshire Playhouse in Leeds) which gives them a fantastic platform to feel brilliant about that final performance moment. Their performance isn't judged in a competitive way, where there is a winner at the end, nor is it critiqued for its professional, theatrical quality. We regard performance simply as a moment to celebrate the end of a much longer and often challenging process that these pupils and their teachers have been through.

The message we give to the teachers is that, if you're going to put on a play, the best resource you have is not the words of Shakespeare, but your pupils and using them to tell the story in their own imaginative and creative way. It is lovely to see how these 400 year-old stories get re-appropriated by the pupils based on the lives that they live. We encourage teachers to ask them questions like "What do you think this means?", "What do you picture when you hear those words?" and "How would you say it?" so that they put on the play in a way that is their own unique re-telling of the story.

We worked with a special primary school in Newcastle this year that did an abridged performance of A Midsummer Night's Dream, alongside a production by another school. The performance the primary school did was very, very beautiful. It was wonderfully simple in that they just chose to tell a quick story about the forest scene from the play. At the end, there was this hushed moment and I thought "Huh! Nobody is clapping!" Then the audience erupted into huge applause! I think what made it so moving was because it was so unexpected to see eight year-olds with downs syndrome on stage, performing Shakespeare. The way in which their teacher worked with them throughout the performance was also very inspiring. He took on the role of telling the story, whilst his pupils acted it out. However, if at any point his pupils felt the urge to start telling the story with him, he would step back and they would step forward and start to tell it - a wonderful, live negotiation of creativity.

We often hear teachers say "You don't know my pupils – they couldn't do that." I believe that this comes from the fear of the teacher who is actually saying "I don't know how to make my students do that." Most of the fear that both teachers and pupils have is of how others will judge them. This fear of judgement and pursuit of perfection is the main thing that gets in the way. I think some competition can be healthy, but striving to be perfect, or worrying that they're not going to be perfect, because the school up the road is renowned for putting on the best plays, simply stops people from trying. Youngsters at primary school are much easier to get going creatively as they can easily tap into the sort of playground mentality of 'lets pretend' because they have more spontaneous access to their imagination as they're still regularly playing those games. There is a palpable shift with teenagers though, who are much more conscious of their bodies, their sexuality, politics (with a small p) and how they interact with each other so these fears start to inhibit their creativity.

In my first year with SSF I was at a big theatre in the north of England and a number of schools had just performed. We asked the Head of Education of the theatre to give an appraisal of the performances. An appraisal comes with a very specific caveat – it is not about judging, it is about giving all of the students that have performed some praise, so that every school has had something positive said about them. At the end of the night she was effusive in talking about the perfect performance of one particular school, which, if you were to judge it as a moment of traditional theatre, was good. She then turned to a company of much younger pupils whose performance of Romeo and Juliet wasn't as theatrically 'good' and simply said to them "I think you can really learn from the other pupils that have been on here tonight - they really showed you how it can be done properly!" It was at that moment I realised why I wanted to do this work – because it's in absolute opposition to people like her, who believe performance, assessment and achieving excellence are the only things that are important. She was totally unappreciative of the process those students had been through: the endless rehearsals they'd been in, those moments at home learning

their lines with their parents, the relationship they have had with their teacher – she crushed all of that with that one awful statement.

We recently worked with a pupil referral unit and, because of the complex personal circumstances of many of the pupils, we knew some of them wouldn't turn up for the performance. We therefore decided to film the entire process that they went through and showed it on the night. It didn't really matter that only two or three pupils turned up because, through showing the video, we made the process the performance. The audience could actually see students wrangling with language and getting annoyed with each other. One student in particular got cross and exclaimed, "I don't understand this language" and walked out of the classroom. However, on the night, he came on stage and performed his own rap inspired by Romeo and Juliet. By making the process the performance, the audience were able to witness that student's creative light bulb moment where he realised how he could make the play his own. Had we just had him on stage performing a rap it would have been nowhere near as inspiring and impactful.

Sona Pattni – The spirit of "yes"

Sona is a final-year student studying Business Management at Aston University. She has always considered herself a creative person, but had noticed she was separating her creativity from her work as she embarked on a year-long placement with a large multi-national organisation. She decided to experiment during her placement.

I always put the pressure on by telling myself I must get everything right first time. I must be perfect, especially as I'm now working in an organisation. However I have found learning to fail happy is actually a lot of fun! One example was a project that I undertook to establish some performance metrics. I'd worked really hard trying to get the formulae on the Excel spread sheet perfected but when my boss had a look at it she quickly pointed out that I hadn't got it right. My old self would have said "Oh no, I'm really bad and should have got that right" but this time I realised my mistake and told myself that it wasn't that bad and that I'd get it right next time because I'd learnt something. I was surprised as I wasn't actually as sad as I thought I would be at failing.

I've experimented with saying "yes" more to the extent I almost felt like I was in the movie "Yes Man"[3]. I started saying "yes" to practically anything. I got an e-mail inviting me to join a society, so I clicked yes and ended up at the Women's Leadership Initiative in London. This was a really unusual experience for me because they did a whole bunch of weird experiments and, although I felt like I wasn't really in tune with the overall theme of the conference, it was fun and I walked

away with a memory I wouldn't have had if I'd said "no". I walked from the WLI workshop with ideas of how I could be more assertive in the workplace, which has already had an impact in what I'm doing now. I also said "yes" to a colleague who wanted help with training her Industrial Placement student and, even though I was incredibly busy at the time, I said "yes". Allthough this meant more workload it didn't feel like a burden because of the spirit in which I said "yes". Normally, I would have grudgingly said "ok then" which would have made it feel like a chore. Again this led to further possibilities where I started to train whole groups of Industrial Placements which was fun and resulted in some great feedback to take with me into the future – feedback I would never have known had I not said "yes."

I still do have moments of questioning myself though. If I say "yes" to something I've never done and I get it wrong, I feel there is a possibility I may be perceived as bad. However I realise that if I say "no" then there is more likelihood of me being perceived as bad for not accepting the offer in the first place. But then, if I "say" yes I could end up being perceived as wrong! I found this really difficult to begin with as I'm not used to it. When you grow up you're not used to the words 'fail' and 'happy' being in the same sentence. I became used to having the words 'fail' and 'bad' in the same sentence, so to alter my mind-set was quite difficult. As I experimented though, I got more comfortable with it and started to fail happy a lot more. I found that if there are more negative consequences it makes it harder to fail happy, but I think what really helped was when I started to see the silver-lining around that really dark grey cloud - that's what really helped me to see the happy side of things. When I fail I'm waiting for that

moment when things rise again knowing that something good will come out of it and I'm learning how to patiently wait for it.

A recent example was an assignment that I got a result back for. I was hoping for a first but it came back as a 2:1, just eight points off a first. Normally I'd be really, really gutted and to some extent I was, but I saw the silver-lining and thought at least I've got a 62. When I told my friends about the result and they saw how happy I was they said "You're mad! The Sona we know thinks about it and gets really angry!" I explained to them that I had spoken with my tutor who had given me some great feedback for future assignments. I was happy because I was grateful I had made the mistakes now and not in my final year where it would have really mattered.

Mike Burnett – Making Others Look Good

Mike is an OD consultant and a soon-to-be graduate of the Positive Organization Development Graduate program at Case Western Reserve University. Mike decided to focus on the practice of Making Others Look Good to expand his change and leadership abilities in support of his ambition to make the world a better place.

Making others look good is a practice that comes more naturally to me. I constantly look for the strengths of other people and also for ways in which they can play to those strengths more often. Whether it's a work project, meaningful conversation, observed random act of kindness or something else, I try to make sure I take note of the positive contributions

others make and call attention to what I observe. Depending on the person, that recognition may be done in public or in private. I try to make sure that people are aware of the positive things I see them do.

My primary motive is to make sure they know that someone saw them do something great and it's amazing to feel the impact on myself when I take the time to notice and recognise the goodness in others. More often than not, people comment that the recognition is greatly appreciated, and you can see them light up when you explain how their contribution made a difference. I believe that everyone wants to feel that they matter and recognition is an ideal way of ensuring this happens. I often saw this practice coming into play while facilitating communication skills training classes at my previous organisation. In each of the classes I facilitated, one of the bi-products of the experience would inevitably be a growing appreciation in each participant of at least one other participant. Because these classes included a representative sample of associates from all parts of the organisation I often took it upon myself to provide people with the space to share their best traits. This practice almost always resulted in increased awareness, acceptance, and appreciation between class participants.

Now it would be naïve to ignore the existence of challenges with the practice of making others look good. I'm sure that all of us have encountered people who just make it difficult to make them look good. In those cases, I try to frame (or re-frame) my perspective around my personal belief that all people contain innately good, wholesome characteristics. If you choose to believe that those difficult people are the way they are as a result of their conditioning, it becomes easier to have compassion for them. It makes it easier to demonstrate empathy for them and to seek out and showcase their positive strengths.

Making others look good is a key aspect of leadership. The practice also aids team development and can be a great source of renewal for the person putting the practice into use. Making this practice a part of your daily routine helps you build relationships and help you become a leader people will follow.

Chapter 10 References

1 The Creative Practice die is a do-it-yourself die that has each of the creative practices written on each side. One rolls it to generate a new creative experiment. You can download one by clicking on the Creative Resources link at www.stevechapman.org

2 Dr Seuss (1954) "*Horton Hears a Who.*" Random House Children's Books

3 "Yes Man" (2008) Directed by Peyton Reed, based on the book by Danny Wallace (2006)

Chapter 11　Beautiful Imperfection

"Have no fear of perfection – you'll never reach it."
Salvador Dali (1904-1989)

I wish I could draw like a six year-old. It is a personal development goal that I take very seriously. People who know me are often puzzled by this rather odd developmental objective. *"Of course you can draw like a 6 year-old"* they try to reassure  me *"your drawings are good."* Whilst this positive encouragement is nice to hear I have to disagree with its validity. I simply can't draw like a 6 year-old because I am 40! I no longer engage with the world in the same way that a 6 year old does and, no matter how hard I try, I no longer have a 6 year-old *eye*. A 6 year-old has learnt just enough to draw things that are recognisable but has not yet been sucked into complying with the social expectations of what *good* art should look like – they simply draw the way in which they see the world.

As mentioned way back in Chapter 1, my own 6 year-old daughter is my creativity mentor and *Chief of Imagination* for *Can Scorpions Smoke?* She regularly produces a stream of artistic masterpieces for me to use in my work and she had a lot of fun providing the illustrations for this book. I am often also treated to musical compositions, plays and improvised games all of which bring me much joy and make me feel truly alive. Whilst there is of course a proud-parent bias in how I view my daughter's work, I have come to realise that my obsession with the style of her creations isn't solely because I am her father. There is something about the quality of her work and the work of most children that fascinates me. A quality I have come to call *beautiful imperfection* - a way of expressing oneself that is exceptionally beautiful because of, not in spite of, its flaws.

It seems to me that, as adults, we devote a lot of our time and energy to ironing out imperfections, rounding any rough edges in order to attain faultlessness due to a shared social belief that this is what the world demands of us. Ironically, it is this need for perfection that stifles the creative spirit of the average human being and inhibits us from giving the world our greatest work. We often don't begin something, or begin but give up trying because we have no guarantee of perfection. Alternatively, we strive so hard to achieve perfection that we burn up lots of energy and fall out of love with whatever it is we are trying to achieve.

I am suspicious that the pursuit of perfection is a waste of time, energy and spirit and that we lose something deeply human in the process of doing so. *In "Orbiting the Giant Hairball"[1]* Gordon MacKenzie talks about peaches and how he noticed that the ones he ate as an adult were more aesthetically perfect than those he remembered in his childhood. He suggests that modern peaches have become "*Hi-tech*". They are perfectly round, perfectly coloured and, rather curiously, have lost virtually all of the *peach fuzz* that he fondly remembered encountering as a child. Gordon suggests that, whilst modern peaches have become more aesthetically pleasing, they have simultaneously lost the explosion of messy, intense flavour that they used to have. He suggests that these super-peaches are an example of how our obsession with perfection can end up reducing the sensuousness of our human experience.

The Beautifully Imperfect Adventurer

I want to end this book on the subject of beautiful imperfection as I am all too aware of the tyranny of perfection when it comes to the development of our creative spirit.
Perfection can dishearten the newly motivated Creative Adventurer when our experiences and results of our experiments do not match our own or society's perception of what success looks like. It is with this in mind that the concept of beautiful imperfection has become very important to me in the time it has taken me to write this book. Many times I have read what I have written and become incredibly frustrated that parts of it don't make sense or contradict other parts or that there is not perfect thread that joins it all up. I've written extra chapters that neaten it all up and edited and re-edited it to give a more polished message and flow in order to appeal more to a corporate audience and convince publishers that people will buy it.

However, realising I was genetically engineering out my own imperfections in order to please others I reverted back to older, messier, experimental drafts for the final version. (This felt like trading a perfectly round peach that would appeal to many for a rather misshapen but juicy one that I hope might appeal to a few.) Similarly, when looking for a publisher, I resisted those who wanted to iron out the creases and neaten it all up for me and make it feel more like a perfect business book. This is why I eventually decided to self publish. The process of writing and producing my first book in this way feels like a big risk but I have decided to practice what I preach and do it anyway as part of my own personal experimentation and adventure. What you hold in your hands today is the result. It is imperfect but hopefully beautiful through proudly being so.

As you continue on your own Creative Adventures I encourage you to gently let go of any ideas you may have of what perfection looks like. In fact let go of any idea of what great or good looks like and simply enjoy the sensuousness of the experience. Take great pride in your experimentation, no matter how big or small. Embrace any flaws that your experiments show up and proudly flaunt them in front of others as they are something as uniquely you as your fingerprints.

Beautiful imperfection is about seeing flaws as an undeniable expression of what it means to be a human being. It is about regarding our own imperfections not as a weakness but as a unique gift that has the power to inspire others. Is it about gently letting go of the tyranny of perfection, certainty and control and embracing a way of being that is compassionately and beautifully imperfect.

Happy adventuring.

Chapter 11 References

[1] Gordon MacKenzie (1996). *"Orbiting the Giant Hairball: A Corporate Fool's Guide to Surviving with Grace."* New York: Penguin Group

Post-script: So Can Scorpions Smoke?

Our ref: **IAS 2011-1969**

Dear Mr Chapman,

Thank you for contacting The Natural History Museum.

The answer to your question is no, scorpions can't smoke.
A large scorpion would be able to physically a) grab a
cigarette in its pincers and b) move it towards its
mouth. For more details about scorpion anatomy and names
for body parts, please read Wikipedia article here:
http://en.wikipedia.org/wiki/Scorpion#Anatomy

However, the scorpion wouldn't be able to c) inhale and
exhale smoke from the cigarette, because scorpions have a
different respiratory system than ours. The 'lungs'
(please see Wikipedia article for book lungs here:
http://en.wikipedia.org/wiki/Book_lung) are situated in
the abdomen, not in the cephalothorax. They don't
communicate with the mouth. Scorpions don't inhale
anyway, as the insects do inflating and deflating their
abdomen. The book lungs work fine without a ventilation
system.

I hope you will find this information useful.

Best wishes,

Florin Feneru
Identification and Advisory Service
Angela Marmont Centre for UK Biodiversity
The Natural History Museum
Cromwell Road, London
SW7 5BD, U.K.
+44 (0)20 7942 5045
ias2@nhm.ac.uk

Big Thanks

This book has only come about through listening to others, asking them what they think and feel and getting them to participate in a variety of unusual experiments. I have named the major influences up front in the introduction to this book, so this page is for everyone else, without whom, the book would have never come to fruition. I am eternally grateful to the following for their help, support and encouragement...

Amelia Morris, Katy Bateson, Gary Aldam, Jennifer Lopez, Sona Pattni, Stuart Harrison, Mike Burnett, Ola Odumosu and Dom Fitch for generously sharing their stories of Creative Adventure with the wider world. My tutors and mentors at Ashridge Business School who helped me to start this journey: Professor Bill Critchley, Caryn Vanstone, Kathleen King, Hugh Pidgeon, Kamil Kelner, Kevin Power and Sarah Beart.

To a collection of important people who continually inspire me by simply hanging out and chatting with them: James Wilson, Lizzie Palmer, Lucy Taylor, Gary Hirsch, Patricia Shaw, Asher Rickayzen, Claire Genkai Breeze, Roger Taylor, Eric Gower and the students of the Case Western Reserve MPOD programme. To those who have played a role as a mentor or trusted advisor to me over the years: Adrian Machon, Sally Bonneywell, Mee-Yan Cheung Judge and Phil Mix. To John-Paul Flintoff for co-creating some crazy ideas and helping me navigate this new world of publishing. To Caroline Sharley who was my performance partner in the Can Scorpions Smoke? origins scene. To every one of the 100 people who contributed to the Giraffe Project.

To the publishers who, through rejecting this book helped me find the unique niche that it now sits in. To those who read and fedback on early drafts, giving me the encouragement and challenge to keep going throughout the process: Khurshed Denhugara, Robert Poynton, Steve Beach and Alison Godfrey. To the late Gordon MacKenzie who I sadly never got to meet but who's own personal masterpiece inspired me to pick up a pen.

And finally to my little family. My wife Kathryn for reading endless drafts of the book, for her expert proof-reading and for believing in me and sticking by me when I left a 'proper' job and stepped into the unknown. A final thank you to my daughter Maya whose own creative spirit inspired me to write it in the first place and who brought the book to life with her wonderful illustrations.

About the author

Steve is fascinated by human beings and how they interact, fall out, make up, change and create stuff together. He is particularly interested in how all of this happens in the workplace and how organisations *really* work as opposed to how they are *supposed* to work.

Having previously spent over 20 years in the corporate world as a senior Leadership & Organisation Development Director for a major blue-chip, he decided to follow his own spirit of adventure and set out as an independent change and creativity consultant, bringing an exciting mix of experience and experimentation to his work. He has worked with a wide variety of clients in the pharmaceutical, FMCG, financial services, digital, telecoms, retail, airlines, utilities, forestry, legal, retail, energy, arts, regulatory, academic and charity sectors helping them through times of change and developing their own creative and innovative spirit.

He holds an MSc with distinction in Organisational Change from Ashridge Business School, where he returns as visiting faculty to talk about organisational change, creativity and innovation. He is also a graduate of the esteemed NTL Organisation Development Programme and a qualified coach, specialising in designing and facilitating experiential 1:1 Creative Adventures for individuals from all walks of life.

He is a regular speaker on the subject of change and creativity and writes a popular blog on the subject.

He is a husband and a Daddy and his six-year-old daughter is his creative mentor and Chief of Imagination at Can Scorpions Smoke Change and Creativity Limited.

You can read more about Steve, his work and his blog at www.stevechapman.org and follow him on Twitter @stevexoh.